# Survey of American Poetry

Volume IX
World War II & Aftermath
1940-1950

# Poetry Anthology Press

### The World's Best Poetry

### Survey of American Poetry

# Survey of American Poetry

## Volume IX
## World War II & Aftermath
## 1940-1950

Prepared by
The Editorial Board, Roth Publishing, Inc.
(formerly Granger Book Co., Inc.)

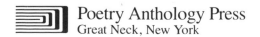 Poetry Anthology Press
Great Neck, New York

The acknowledgements on pages 307-309 constitute a continuation of this copyright notice.

Library of Congress Catalog Card Number 81-83526
International Standard Book Number 0-89609-221-6
International Standard Book Number for
Foundation Volumes I-X, 0-89609-299-2

Manufactured in the U.S.A.

Poetry Anthology Press is a
division of Roth Publishing, Inc.
(formerly Granger Book Co., Inc.)

# CONTENTS

# Preface

The publications of **Poetry Anthology Press** constitute a comprehensive conspectus of international verse in English designed to form the core of a library's poetry collection. Covering the entire range of poetic literature, these anthologies encompass all topics and national literatures.

Each collection, published in a multivolume continuing series format, is devoted to a major area of the whole undertaking and contains complete author, title, and first line indexes. Biographical data is also provided.

*The World's Best Poetry,* with coverage through the 19th century, is topically classified and arranged by subject matter. Supplements keep the 10 volume foundation collection current and complete.

*Survey of American Poetry* is an anthology of American verse arranged chronologically in 10 volumes. Each volume presents a significant period of American poetic history, from 1607 to date.

# INTRODUCTION

The years 1940 to 1950 constitute a period of profound significance, not only in American history but in world history as well. World War II (1939-1945) was the bloodiest, costliest war ever fought. Not only did the war exact a hellish toll on the lives of military personnel and civilians, but, through a program of systematic genocide, the Germans–a people renowned for their learning and culture–put millions to their death. Moreover, with the development of the atomic bomb in July of 1945, the notion of species-wide genocide became a chilling possibility. American poets who came to maturity at this time were distinguished from the previous generation by their introspection and their skeptical view of received values and morality. These poets saw the world as a dangerous, chaotic place and, in response, they retreated inward, searching for meaning through an exhaustive exploration of the self. If one is to fully appreciate the verse of this time, it is important to have a general understanding of the events that shaped and motivated it.

World War II officially started in Europe on September 1, 1939, with the German blitzkrieg of Poland, yet it would be more than two years before the United States joined the fighting. While U.S. sympathies were with the Allied forces from the start, the terrible memory of the First World War lingered, and Americans were anxious to maintain a neutral posture lest they once again become involved in a European conflict. At the same time, Japan was in poor standing with the U.S. and had been since its invasion of China in 1937. In response to that act of aggression, America had severed commercial ties with Japan and provided war materials to China. The global situation grew graver still in April of 1940, as German troops moved into Norway and Denmark and, soon thereafter, invaded Holland, Belgium, Luxembourg, and France. Previously, Congress had taken an isolationist stand in foreign affairs, passing a series of neutrality laws in the late thirties; but now, in view of Nazi aggression, it designated large amounts of money to the military in order to ensure America's preparedness for war.

This was the setting in 1940 when Franklin D. Roosevelt defeated Republican Wendell L. Wilkie in the Presidential election, thereby winning an unprecedented third term in office. At this time, the U.S. abandoned its posture of neutrality and declared itself the "arsenal of democracy"; vast quantities of military supplies were sent to England, and U.S. forces occupied both Greenland and Iceland in order to keep important trade routes open. Tensions continued to mount as German troops poured into the U.S.S.R. in June of 1941. (Russia had hitherto been aligned with Germany in a non-aggression pact, but now the U.S. and England were fast to offer her aid.) In October, a German submarine sank a U.S. destroyer and the navy was ordered thenceforward to shoot on sight.

Meanwhile, General Tojo, Japan's premier, had sent representatives to Washington in an attempt to iron out difficulties between the two nations. However, on December 7, 1941, while the negotiations were still in progress, the Japanese launched their devastating surprise attack on Pearl Harbor, effectively crippling U.S. naval operations in the Pacific. Of course there could now be no more thought of avoiding direct participation in the war; one day later, Congress declared war against Japan and, on December 11, Japan and her allies, the Axis nations (Germany and Italy), made a similar declaration against the U.S.

A long series of Japanese victories in the Pacific followed Pearl Harbor and, indeed, it was not until June of 1942, with the battle of Midway Island, that the U.S. began to curb the Japanese advance. Decisive victories against the Axis powers were scored in North Africa and Italy in the middle of the following year and, on June 6, 1944, the famous "D-Day" invasion was launched by U.S. and British forces in Normandy. On August 25, Paris was liberated, and by October the Germans had been removed from French soil. The Battle of the Bulge (Belgium and Luxembourg) in December of 1944 was the Germans' last offensive, but their success was short-lived, as Allied troops pushed west, while the Russians approached from the east. The two forces met at the Elbe River in April of 1945 and, on May 7, the Germans acceded to the Allied demand for "unconditional surrender."

By this time, Roosevelt had died (he had been elected to a fourth term in 1944), and it fell upon Harry S. Truman to deal with the Japanese. In June of 1945, American troops took over Okinawa, a strategic island on the outskirts of Japan; however, in view of the tenacity of the Japanese soldiers, the occupation of the rest of the country promised to be a long and costly undertaking. It was with this in mind that Truman ordered the dropping of atomic bombs on Hiroshima and Nagasaki, respectively, on August 6 and 9 of that year. It was Truman's belief that even though hundreds of thousands would be incinerated in these blasts, the loss of life would still be less than that incurred in a drawn-out conventional war. About 150,000 were killed or injured in Hiroshima alone, as the explosion burned out 4.4 square miles of the city and destroyed about two-thirds of its 90,000 homes. On September 2, the Japanese formally surrendered.

In America, civilians had performed admirably in aiding the war effort. Indeed, many historians agree that U.S. supremacy in war production was the key to the Allied victory. After Pearl Harbor, industries were put on a round-the-clock schedule, and over two-million women were added to the work force in place of the men who joined the armed services. Less than a year after Pearl Harbor, U.S. war production equalled that of all the Axis nations combined; by early 1943, it had eclipsed Axis production. War agencies were set up in the U.S. to monitor crucial areas of the economy such as labor, housing, transportation, and manpower; an Office of Censorship was created with the power to censor all communications with other countries. In September of 1942, Congress granted Roosevelt the power to freeze consumer prices, salaries, and wages, and, in July of the following year, all rents were frozen as well. Though Americans suffered little in comparison with those in whose countries the fighting took place, they contended with the rationing of coffee, tea, sugar, butter, gasoline, and meats. They also contributed to the war effort through paying increased taxes and buying war bonds.

By the time it had run its course, World War II had become the costliest, most devastating war in history. It is estimated that about 15 to 20 million military personnel lost their lives during the war (almost 300,000 Americans). Civilian casualties are harder to assess, but experts put the total near 25 million, and economically the war cost some $1,154,000,000,000. If anything good can be said to have come out of the war, one might point to the formation of the United Nations, which officially came into being on October 24, 1945. World leaders realized that the failure to institute such a body after World War I was a mistake they did not want to repeat. Special organizations were set up under U.N. auspices to deal with agriculture, health, monetary problems, etc., and, in the next several years, the U.N. succeeded in settling disputes between Iran and Russia, the East Indies and the Dutch, and India and Pakistan.

In the aftermath of the War, Harry Truman found the country gravitating far to the right of the liberal course formerly pursued by Roosevelt. Americans were tired of the hardships of the war years and looked to the

Republican party for relief. In 1946 Republicans gained control of Congress for the first time in sixteen years. Thus, while Truman was able to hold onto the presidency by his startling 1948 upset of Thomas Dewey, he was unable to implement his "Fair Deal" program (essentially an extension of Roosevelt's "New Deal"). Public opinion gradually turned against labor, which was perceived as being too powerful. Truman's attempts to establish a national health insurance program were foiled–as was a civil rights program–by a powerful Congressional coalition between Republicans and conservative southern Democrats. Mindful of the threat of Soviet expansionism, the U.S. formed an alliance with the countries of western Europe (the North Atlantic Treaty Organization). Yet despite his deep concern with the threat of Communism, Truman opposed the McCarran Act, which required the registration of all Communists and their organizations. The growing fear of the left in America was to culminate in the following decade with McCarthyism.

Some link the increasingly conservative political climate of the forties with a commensurate change in the poetry of the time, which seemed to retreat from the rampant experimentalism of the three previous decades. By now the modernist movement in verse, which had been spearheaded by such figures as Ezra Pound, T.S. Eliot, and William Carlos Williams, was so widely accepted as to have all but lost its revolutionary character. With the nineteenth century fading ever further from memory, there was no longer the need to cast oneself as a "modern," twentieth century poet. Furthermore, "institutionalization" had cooled the radical fervor of modernism, as poets gravitated to the nation's universities. Whereas in the past a poet might have supported him- or herself as a journalist, a freelance writer, or by simply doing odd jobs, now poets began turning up on English department faculties. (Almost every poet in this anthology was affiliated with an institution of higher learning at some point in his or her career; indeed, Theodore Roethke, Randall Jarrell, Josephine Miles, Owen Dodson, and Paul Goodman were professors throughout their adult lives.) As a result, experimental verse was no longer the province of small circles of bohemians in London or Greenwich Village, but rather it was taught and advocated in colleges across the country. By 1940 the broadest objectives of modernist verse had been accomplished: the stilted, overly-poetic diction of the past had given way to concise, exacting, idiomatic language; poets and their audiences were comfortable with non-rhyming poems in open forms; and poets were free to address virtually any subject matter in their verse. In view of these accomplishments, many poets were again attracted to traditional verse forms, albeit with the intention of revitalizing them through the lessons learned from the modernists.

There also arose in the forties a difficult, "academic" poetry. When one considers the union of poet and university at this time and the continued eminence of learned poets like Pound and Eliot, this development is not surprising. New Criticism, a critical movement that prized close textual analysis and rejected historical and biographical information as extraneous, held sway in the thirties and forties and inculcated its practitioners with a taste for complex poems distinguished by ambiguity, irony, and metaphysical wit. John Berryman, Theodore Roethke, and Robert Lowell are some notable figures who wrote in this manner.

However, of all the influences exerted on poetry during this period, World War II had the most profound effect. The devastation of the war was without parallel in human history, and, with the development of the atomic bomb, humanity faced the almost unimaginable thought that it was capable of destroying itself and the world. Any poet that lived through the war could not help but respond; however, to posit a single, representative reaction among postwar poets would be to oversimplify, for one of the hallmarks of American verse from 1940 onward is its multiplicity. Randall Jarrell and Karl Shapiro both produced powerful poems out of their experiences in the war; Brother Antoninus (William Everson) and Robert Lowell, as conscientious objectors, both refused military service and were subsequently imprisoned. By and large, American poets were unable to view World War II as anything but a terrible insanity; they were unwilling to indulge in a misplaced patriotism that exulted in the Allied victory, for too much had been lost on both sides. Many adopted the existentialist view that one is alone in an indifferent, amoral universe, and, more than ever before, the postwar poets began to explore the self–the only terrain they felt could be "known" in any real sense. Brother Antoninus and Robert Lowell, in his later career, are apt examples of this impulse. Lowell came to be known as "the leader of the Confessional school."

Perhaps the growing political conservatism of these years also had something to do with this poetic shift inward. The thirties, owing to the social reforms of Roosevelt's "New Deal" program, had a distinctly socialistic air; among intellectual circles, leftist radicalism was so prevalent that the period had been dubbed "the Red Decade" by some. With America's subsequent shift to the right, the egalitarian mood dissipated, and poetry became less political and more personal.

In the internationalist spirit of Pound and Eliot, poets attempted to go beyond their own American-British traditions and expand themselves and their work through the study of new literatures and cultures; this endeavor was aided by the proliferation of translations then appearing. However, the key to the multiplicity of the verse of the forties (and thereafter) is the poet's increased concern with the self. The act of writing poetry became a search for a voice and manner of one's own, an exercise in self-definition. And perhaps this is also the key to the attraction this poetry holds for us today: it is a poetry of individuals and, together as a body of literature, it is as rich and varied as humanity itself.

# EXPLANATORY NOTES

The present anthology is arranged chronologically. Its aim is (a) to provide the reader with a sense of the development of verse during the historical period and (b) to help place select works within the span of each poet's creative output. Accordingly, it lists the poets in sequence—by date of birth—and, wherever possible, gives the date of individual poems.

Words are spelled as they appear in the original sources; punctuation, capitalization, and usage are treated the same way. No attempt has been made to reconcile resulting inconsistencies. This, however, should not hinder a basic appreciation of the material. In some cases, the poems entered constitute selections; these are chosen to convey to the reader the essence of a major work which is too long to publish in the context of the anthology.

Authors, titles, and first lines are arranged in a single alphabetical listing in the Index. Poet names are in boldface; poem titles are in italics; and poem first lines are enclosed in quotation marks. When a title and first line are identical, only the title is given.

# KENNETH REXROTH   [1905-1982]

Though born in South Bend, Indiana, Kenneth Rexroth grew up in Chicago. Mostly self-educated, he quit school when he was sixteen and spent his early years trying various jobs, some of which included: logger, newspaper reporter, and labor organizer. He then moved to San Francisco where he lived for many years, actively participating in the city's lively poetic scene. Throughout his career, Rexroth took a generous interest in the efforts of younger poets, particularly those of the Black Mountain school and the Beat movement. Rexroth wrote frequently of the beauties of the California landscape, and, indeed, his mountain poems stand as some of the finest examples of poems about nature in the language. He also wrote critical essays and produced translations from no less than six languages, including ancient Greek and Chinese.

*Andrée Rexroth*

Mt. Tamalpais

The years have gone. It is spring
Again. Mars and Saturn will
Soon come on, low in the West,
In the dusk. Now the evening
Sunlight makes hazy girders
Over Steep Ravine above
The waterfalls. The winter
Birds from Oregon, robins
And varied thrushes, feast on
Ripe toyon and madrone
Berries. The robins sing as
The dense light falls.
                         Your ashes
Were scattered in this place. Here
I wrote you a farewell poem,
And long ago another,
A poem of peace and love,
Of the lassitude of a long
Spring evening in youth. Now
It is almost ten years since
You came here to stay. Once more,
The pussy willows that come
After the New Year in this
Outlandish land are blooming.
There are deer and raccoon tracks
In the same places. A few
New sand bars and cobble beds
Have been left where erosion
Has gnawed deep into the hills.
The rounds of life are narrow.
War and peace have past like ghosts.
The human race sinks towards
Oblivion. A bittern
Calls from the same rushes where
You heard one on our first year

In the West; and where I heard
One again in the year
Of your death.

### Kings River Canyon

My sorrow is so wide
I cannot see across it;
And so deep I shall never
Reach the bottom of it.
The moon sinks through deep haze,
As though the Kings River Canyon
Were filled with fine, warm, damp gauze.
Saturn gleams through the thick light
Like a gold, wet eye; nearby,
Antares glows faintly,
Without sparkle. Far overhead,
Stone shines darkly in the moonlight—
Lookout Point, where we lay
In another full moon, and first
Peered down into this canyon.
Here we camped, by still autumnal
Pools, all one warm October.
I baked you a bannock birthday cake.
Here you did your best paintings—
Innocent, wondering landscapes.
Very few of them are left
Anywhere. You destroyed them
In the terrible trouble
Of your long sickness. Eighteen years
Have passed since that autumn.
There was no trail here then.
Only a few people knew
How to enter this canyon.
We were all alone, twenty
Miles from anybody;
A young husband and wife,
Closed in and wrapped about
In the quiet autumn,

In the sound of quiet water,
In the turning and falling leaves,
In the wavering of innumerable
Bats from the caves, dipping
Over the odorous pools
Where the great trout drowsed in the evenings.
Eighteen years have been ground
To pieces in the wheels of life.
You are dead. With a thousand
Convicts they have blown a highway
Through Horseshoe Bend. Youth is gone,
That only came once. My hair
Is turning grey and my body
Heavier. I too move on to death.
I think of Henry King's stilted
But desolated *Exequy*,
Of Yuan Chen's great poem,
Unbearably pitiful;
Alone by the Spring river
More alone than I had ever
Imagined I would ever be,
I think of Frieda Lawrence,
Sitting alone in New Mexico,
In the long drought, listening
For the hiss of the milky Isar,
Over the cobbles, in a lost Spring.


*Climbing Milestone Mountain,*
*August 22, 1937*


For a month now, wandering over the Sierras,
A poem had been gathering in my mind,
Details of significance and rhythm,
The way poems do, but still lacking a focus.
Last night I remembered the date and it all
Began to grow together and take on purpose.
   We sat up late while Deneb moved over the zenith
And I told Marie all about Boston, how it looked

That last terrible week, how hundreds stood weeping
Impotent in the streets that last midnight.
I told her how those hours changed the lives of
    thousands,
How America was forever a different place
Afterwards for many.
                    In the morning
We swam in the cold transparent lake, the blue
Damsel flies on all the reeds like millions
Of narrow metallic flowers, and I thought
Of you behind the grille in Dedham, Vanzetti,
Saying, "Who would ever have thought we would
    make this history?"
Crossing the brilliant mile-square meadow
Illuminated with asters and cyclamen,
The pollen of the lodgepole pines drifting
With the shifting wind over it and the blue
And sulphur butterflies drifting with the wind,
I saw you in the sour prison light, saying,
"Goodbye comrade."
                    In the basin under the crest
Where the pines end and the Sierra primrose begins,
A party of lawyers was shooting at a whiskey bottle.
The bottle stayed on its rock, nobody could hit it.
Looking back over the peaks and canyons from the
    last lake,
The pattern of human beings seemed simpler
Than the diagonals of water and stone.
Climbing the chute, up the melting snow and broken
    rock,
I remembered what you said about Sacco,
How it slipped your mind and you demanded it be
    read into the record.
Traversing below the ragged arête,
One cheek pressed against the rock
The wind slapping the other,
I saw you both marching in an army
You with the red and black flag, Sacco with the
    rattlesnake banner.

I kicked steps up the last snow bank and came
To the indescribably blue and fragrant
Polemonium and the dead sky and the sterile
Crystalline granite and final monolith of the summit.
These are the things that will last a long time,
    Vanzetti,
I am glad that once on your day I have stood among
    them.
Some day mountains will be named after you and
    Sacco.
They will be here and your name with them,
"When these days are but a dim remembering of the
    time
When man was wolf to man."
I think men will be remembering you a long time
Standing on the mountains
Many men, a long time, comrade.


### Night below Zero

3 A.M., the night is absolutely still;
Snow squeals beneath my skis, plumes on the turns,
I stop at the canyon's edge, stand looking out
Over the Great Valley, over the millions—
In bed, drunk, loving, tending mills, furnaces,
Alone, wakeful, as the world rolls in chaos.
The quarter moon rises in the black heavens—
Over the sharp constellations of the cities
The cold lies, crystalline and silent,
Locked between the mountains.


### A Sword in a Cloud of Light

Your hand in mine, we walk out
To watch the Christmas Eve crowds
On Fillmore Street, the Negro
District. The night is thick with

Frost. The people hurry, wreathed
In their smoky breaths. Before
The shop windows the children
Jump up and down with spangled
Eyes. Santa Clauses ring bells.
Cars stall and honk. Street cars clang.
Loud speakers on the lampposts
Sing carols, on juke boxes
In the bars Louis Armstrong
Plays *White Christmas*. In the joints
The girls strip and grind and bump
To *Jingle Bells*. Overhead
The neon signs scribble and
Erase and scribble again
Messages of avarice,
Joy, fear, hygiene, and the proud
Names of the middle classes.
The moon beams like a pudding.
We stop at the main corner
And look up, diagonally
Across, at the rising moon,
And the solemn, orderly
Vast winter constellations.
You say, "There's Orion!"
The most beautiful object
Either of us will ever
Know in the world or in life
Stands in the moonlit empty
Heavens, over the swarming
Men, women, and children, black
And white, joyous and greedy,
Evil and good, buyer and
Seller, master and victim,
Like some immense theorem,
Which, if once solved would forever
Solve the mystery and pain
Under the bells and spangles.
There he is, the man of the
Night before Christmas, spread out

On the sky like a true god
In whom it would only be
Necessary to believe
A little. I am fifty
And you are five. It would do
No good to say this and it
May do no good to write it.
Believe in Orion. Believe
In the night, the moon, the crowded
Earth. Believe in Christmas and
Birthdays and Easter rabbits.
Believe in all those fugitive
Compounds of nature, all doomed
To waste away and go out.
Always be true to these things.
They are all there is. Never
Give up this savage religion
For the blood-drenched civilized
Abstractions of the rascals
Who live by killing you and me.

## THEODORE ROETHKE   [1908-1963]

Theodore Roethke was born in Saginaw, Michigan. His father, uncle, and grandfather owned twenty-five acres of land on which they grew flowers. Throughout his life, Roethke vividly remembered the hours he spent as a child in his family's lush, exotic greenhouses–a fact which sheds a good deal of light on his work, especially the early poems. Roethke attended the University of Michigan and later did his graduate work at Harvard. He taught at Lafayette College, Pennsylvania State University, Bennington College and, from 1945 until his death, at the University of Washington. In addition to his reputation as one of the finest and most original poets of his generation (he received the Pulitzer and Bollingen prizes), Roethke has been praised as a sensitive and insightful teacher of verse; among his students are the poets David Wagoner and James Wright. Roethke's personal life, though, was tormented by manic-depression, alcoholism, and a frantic desire for fame. He remarked, however, that he composed some of his best poetry even as he felt a manic period coming on. He was subject to occasional breakdowns, and his long stay at the University of Washington was made possible by that institution's understanding of his troubles. He died in 1963 and, if his total poetic output is rather slim, it is an example of quality compsensating for quantity.

### The Coming of the Cold

#### 1

The late peach yields a subtle musk,
The arbor is alive with fume
More heady than a field at dusk
When clover scents diminished wind.
The walker's foot has scarcely room
Upon the orchard path, for skinned
And battered fruit has choked the grass.
The yield's half down and half in air,
The plum drops pitch upon the ground,
And nostrils widen as they pass
The place where butternuts are found.
The wind shakes out the scent of pear.
Upon the field the scent is dry:
The dill bears up its acrid crown;
The dock, so garish to the eye,
Distills a pungence of its own;
And pumpkins sweat a bitter oil.
But soon cold rain and frost come in
To press pure fragrance to the soil;
The loose vine droops with hoar at dawn,
The riches of the air blow thin.

#### 2

The ribs of leaves lie in the dust,
The beak of frost has picked the bough,
The briar bears its thorn, and drought
Has left its ravage on the field.
The season's wreckage lies about,
Late autumn fruit is rotted now.
All shade is lean, the antic branch
Jerks skyward at the touch of wind,
Dense trees no longer hold the light,
The hedge and orchard grove are thinned.
The dank bark dries beneath the sun,

The last of harvesting is done.
All things are brought to barn and fold.
The oak leaves strain to be unbound,
The sky turns dark, the year grows old,
The buds draw in before the cold.

3

The small brook dies within its bed;
The stem that holds the bee is prone;
Old hedgerows keep the leaves; the phlox,
That late autumnal bloom, is dead.
All summer green is now undone:
The hills are grey, the trees are bare,
The mould upon the branch is dry,
The fields are harsh and bare, the rocks
Gleam sharply on the narrow sight.
The land is desolate, the sun
No longer gilds the scene at noon;
Winds gather in the north and blow
Bleak clouds across the heavy sky,
And frost is marrow-cold, and soon
Winds bring a fine and bitter snow.

*The Auction*

Once on returning home, purse-proud and hale,
I found my choice possessions on the lawn.
An auctioneer was whipping up a sale.
I did not move to claim what was my own.

"One coat of pride, perhaps a bit threadbare;
Illusion's trinkets, splendid for the young;
Some items, miscellaneous, marked 'Fear';
The chair of honor, with a missing rung."

The spiel ran on; the sale was brief and brisk;
The bargains fell to bidders, one by one.
Hope flushed my cheekbones with a scarlet disk.
Old neighbors nudged each other at the fun.

My spirits rose each time the hammer fell,
The heart beat faster as the fat words rolled.
I left my home with unencumbered will
And all the rubbish of confusion sold.

### Lull

#### November, 1939

The winds of hatred blow
Cold, cold across the flesh
And chill the anxious heart;
Intricate phobias grow
From each malignant wish
To spoil collective life.
Now each man stands apart.

We watch opinion drift,
Think of our separate skins.
On well-upholstered bums
The generals cough and shift
Playing with painted pins.
The arbitrators wait;
The newsmen suck their thumbs.
The mind is quick to turn
Away from simple faith
To the cant and fury of
Fools who will never learn;
Reason embraces death,
While out of frightened eyes
Still stares the wish to love.

*Highway: Michigan*

Here from the field's edge we survey
The progress of the jaded. Mile
On mile of traffic from the town
Rides by, for at the end of day
The time of workers is their own.

They jockey for position on
The strip reserved for passing only.
The drivers from production lines
Hold to advantage dearly won.
They toy with death and traffic fines.

Acceleration is their need:
A mania keeps them on the move
Until the toughest nerves are frayed.
They are the prisoners of speed
Who flee in what their hands have made.

The pavement smokes when two cars meet
And steel rips through conflicting steel.
We shiver at the siren's blast.
One driver, pinned beneath the seat,
Escapes from the machine at last.

*Orchids*

They lean over the path,
Adder-mouthed,
Swaying close to the face,
Coming out, soft and deceptive,
Limp and damp, delicate as a young bird's tongue;
Their fluttery fledgling lips
Move slowly,
Drawing in the warm air.

And at night,
The faint moon falling through whitewashed glass,
The heat going down
So their musky smell comes even stronger,
Drifting down from their mossy cradles:
So many devouring infants!
Soft luminescent fingers,
Lips neither dead nor alive,
Loose ghostly mouths
Breathing.

## Moss-Gathering

To loosen with all ten fingers held wide and limber
And lift up a patch, dark-green, the kind for lining cemetery baskets,
Thick and cushiony, like an old-fashioned doormat,
The crumbling small hollow sticks on the underside mixed with roots,
And wintergreen berries and leaves still stuck to the top,–
That was moss-gathering.
But something always went out of me when I dug loose those carpets
Of green, or plunged to my elbows in the spongy yellowish moss of the
        marshes:
And afterwards I always felt mean, jogging back over the logging road,
As if I had broken the natural order of things in that swampland;
Disturbed some rhythm, old and of vast importance,
By pulling off flesh from the living planet;
As if I had committed, against the whole scheme of life, a desecration.

## Big Wind

Where were the greenhouses going,
Lunging into the lashing
Wind driving water
So far down the river
All the faucets stopped?–
So we drained the manure-machine
For the steam plant,

Pumping the stale mixture
Into the rusty boilers,
Watching the pressure gauge
Waver over to red,
As the seams hissed
And the live steam
Drove to the far
End of the rose-house,
Where the worst wind was,
Creaking the cypress window-frames,
Cracking so much thin glass
We stayed all night,
Stuffing the holes with burlap;
But she rode it out,
That old rose-house,
She hove into the teeth of it,
The core and pith of that ugly storm,
Ploughing with her stiff prow,
Bucking into the wind-waves
That broke over the whole of her,
Flailing her sides with spray,
Flinging long strings of wet across the roof-top,
Finally veering, wearing themselves out, merely
Whistling thinly under the wind-vents;
She sailed until the calm morning,
Carrying her full cargo of roses.


### Transplanting

Watching hands transplanting,
Turning and tamping,
Lifting the young plants with two fingers,
Sifting in a palm-full of fresh loam,–
One swift movement,–
Then plumping in the bunched roots,
A single twist of the thumbs, a tamping and turning,
All in one,
Quick on the wooden bench,

A shaking down, while the stem stays straight,
Once, twice, and a faint third thump,–
Into the flat-box it goes,
Ready for the long days under the sloped glass:

The sun warming the fine loam,
The young horns winding and unwinding,
Creaking their thin spines,
The underleaves, the smallest buds
Breaking into nakedness,
The blossoms extending
Out into the sweet air,
The whole flower extending outward,
Stretching and reaching.


*Frau Bauman, Frau Schmidt, and Frau Schwartze*

Gone the three ancient ladies
Who creaked on the greenhouse ladders,
Reaching up white strings
To wind, to wind
The sweet-pea tendrils, the smilax,
Nasturtiums, the climbing
Roses, to straighten
Carnations, red
Chrysanthemums; the stiff
Stems, jointed like corn,
They tied and tucked,–
These nurses of nobody else.
Quicker than birds, they dipped
Up and sifted the dirt;
They sprinkled and shook;
They stood astride pipes,
Their skirts billowing out wide into tents,
Their hands twinkling with wet;
Like witches they flew along rows
Keeping creation at ease;
With a tendril for needle

They sewed up the air with a stem;
They teased out the seed that the cold kept asleep,–
All the coils, loops, and whorls.
They trellised the sun; they plotted for more than themselves.

I remember how they picked me up, a spindly kid,
Pinching and poking my thin ribs
Till I lay in their laps, laughing,
Weak as a whiffet;
Now, when I'm alone and cold in my bed,
They still hover over me,
These ancient leathery crones,
With their bandannas stiffened with sweat,
And their thorn-bitten wrists,
And their snuff-laden breath blowing lightly over me in my first sleep.

### My Papa's Waltz

The whiskey on your breath
Could make a small boy dizzy;
But I hung on like death:
Such waltzing was not easy.

We romped until the pans
Slid from the kitchen shelf;
My mother's countenance
Could not unfrown itself.

The hand that held my wrist
Was battered on one knuckle;
At every step you missed
My right ear scraped a buckle.

You beat time on my head
With a palm caked hard by dirt,
Then waltzed me off to bed
Still clinging to your shirt.

*The Lost Son*

1. The Flight

At Woodlawn I heard the dead cry:
I was lulled by the slamming of iron,
A slow drip over stones,
Toads brooding wells.
All the leaves stuck out their tongues;
I shook the softening chalk of my bones,
Saying,
Snail, Snail, glister me forward,
Bird, soft-sigh me home,
Worm, be with me.
This is my hard time.

Fished in an old wound,
The soft pond of repose;
Nothing nibbled my line,
Not even the minnows came.

Sat in an empty house
Watching shadows crawl,
Scratching.
There was one fly.

Voice, come out of the silence.
Say something.
Appear in the form of a spider
Or a moth beating the curtain.

Tell me:
Which is the way I take;
Out of what door do I go,
Where and to whom?

Dark hollows said, lee to the wind,
The moon said, back of an eel,
The salt said, look by the sea,

Your tears are not enough praise,
You will find no comfort here,
In the kingdom of bang and blab.

Running lightly over spongy ground,
Past the pasture of flat stones,
The three elms,
The sheep strewn on a field,
Over a rickety bridge
Toward the quick-water, wrinkling and rippling.

Hunting along the river,
Down among the rubbish, the bug-riddled foliage,
By the muddy pond-edge, by the bog-holes,
By the shrunken lake, hunting, in the heat of summer.

The shape of a rat?
    It's bigger than that.
    It's less than a leg
    And more than a nose,
    Just under the water
    It usually goes.

    Is it soft like a mouse?
    Can it wrinkle its nose?
    Could it come in the house
    On the tips of its toes?

    Take the skin of a cat
    And the back of an eel,
    Then roll them in grease,–
    That's the way it would feel.

    It's sleek as an otter
    With wide webby toes
    Just under the water
    It usually goes.

## 2. The Pit

Where do the roots go?
        Look down under the leaves.
Who put the moss there?
        These stones have been here too long.
Who stunned the dirt into noise?
        Ask the mole, he knows.
I feel the slime of a wet nest.
        Beware Mother Mildew.
Nibble again, fish nerves.


## 3. The Gibber

At the wood's mouth,
By the cave's door,
I listened to something
I had heard before.

Dogs of the groin
Barked and howled,
The sun was against me,
The moon would not have me.

The weeds whined,
The snakes cried,
The cows and briars
Said to me: Die.

What a small song. What slow clouds. What dark water.
Hath the rain a father? All the caves are ice. Only the snow's here.
I'm cold. I'm cold all over. Rub me in father and mother.
Fear was my father, Father Fear.
His look drained the stones.

        What gliding shape
        Beckoning through halls,

Stood poised on the stair,
Fell dreamily down?

From the mouths of jugs
Perched on many shelves,
I saw substance flowing
That cold morning.

Like a slither of eels
That watery cheek
As my own tongue kissed
My lips awake.

Is this the storm's heart? The ground is unstilling itself.
My veins are running nowhere. Do the bones cast out their fire?
Is the seed leaving the old bed? These buds are live as birds.
Where, where are the tears of the world?
Let the kisses resound, flat like a butcher's palm;
Let the gestures freeze; our doom is already decided.
All the windows are burning! What's left of my life?
I want the old rage, the lash of primordial milk!
Goodbye, goodbye, old stones, the time-order is going,
I have married my hands to perpetual agitation,
I run, I run to the whistle of money.

Money money money
Water water water

How cool the grass is.
Has the bird left?
The stalk still sways.
Has the worm a shadow?
What do the clouds say?

These sweeps of light undo me.
Look, look, the ditch is running white!
I've more veins than a tree!
Kiss me, ashes, I'm falling through a dark swirl.

## 4. The Return

The way to the boiler was dark,
Dark all the way,
Over slippery cinders
Through the long greenhouse.

The roses kept breathing in the dark.
They had many mouths to breathe with.
My knees made little winds underneath
Where the weeds slept.

There was always a single light
Swinging by the fire-pit,
Where the fireman pulled out roses,
The big roses, the big bloody clinkers.

Once I stayed all night.
The light in the morning came slowly over the white
Snow.
There were many kinds of cool
Air.
Then came steam.

Pipe-knock.

Scurry of warm over small plants.
Ordnung! ordnung!
Papa is coming!

A fine haze moved off the leaves;
Frost melted on far panes;
The rose, the chrysanthemum turned toward the light.
Even the hushed forms, the bent yellowy weeds
Moved in a slow up-sway.

## 5. "It was beginning winter"

It was beginning winter,
An in-between time,
The landscape still partly brown:
The bones of weeds kept swinging in the wind,
Above the blue snow.

It was beginning winter,
The light moved slowly over the frozen field,
Over the dry seed-crowns,
The beautiful surviving bones
Swinging in the wind.

Light travelled over the wide field;
Stayed.
The weeds stopped swinging.
The mind moved, not alone,
Through the clear air, in the silence.

Was it light?
Was it light within?
Was it light within light?
Stillness becoming alive,
Yet still?

A lively understandable spirit
Once entertained you.
It will come again.
Be still.
Wait.

### The Shape of the Fire

1

What's this? A dish for fat lips.
Who says? A nameless stranger.
Is he a bird or a tree? Not everyone can tell.

Water recedes to the crying of spiders.
An old scow bumps over black rocks.
A cracked pod calls.

Mother me out of here. What more will the bones allow?
Will the sea give the wind suck? A toad folds into a stone.
These flowers are all fangs. Comfort me, fury.
Wake me, witch, we'll do the dance of rotten sticks.

Shale loosens. Marl reaches into the field. Small birds pass over water.
Spirit, come near. This is only the edge of whiteness.
I can't laugh at a procession of dogs.

In the hour of ripeness the tree is barren.
The she-bear mopes under the hill.
Mother, mother, stir from your cave of sorrow.

A low mouth laps water. Weeds, weeds, how I love you.
The arbor is cooler. Farewell, farewell, fond worm.
The warm comes without sound.

2

Where's the eye?
The eye's in the sty.
The ear's not here
Beneath the hair.
When I took off my clothes
To find a nose,
There was only one shoe

For the waltz of To,
The pinch of Where.

Time for the flat-headed man. I recognize that listener,
Him with the platitudes and rubber doughnuts,
Melting at the knees, a varicose horror.
Hello, hello. My nerves knew you, dear boy.
Have you come to unhinge my shadow?
Last night I slept in the pits of a tongue.
The silver fish ran in and out of my special bindings;
I grew tired of the ritual of names and the assistant keeper of the
          mollusks:
Up over a viaduct I came, to the snakes and sticks of another winter,
A two-legged dog hunting a new horizon of howls.
The wind sharpened itself on a rock;
A voice sang:

> Pleasure on ground
> Has no sound,
> Easily maddens
> The uneasy man.

> Who, careless, slips
> In coiling ooze
> Is trapped to the lips,
> Leaves more than shoes;

> Must pull off clothes
> To jerk like a frog
> On belly and nose
> From the sucking bog.

My meat eats me. Who waits at the gate?
Mother of quartz, your words writhe into my ear.
Renew the light, lewd whisper.

3

The wasp waits.
    The edge cannot eat the center.
The grape glistens.
    The path tells little to the serpent.
An eye comes out of the wave.
    The journey from flesh is longest.
A rose sways least.
    The redeemer comes a dark way.

4

Morning-fair, follow me further back
Into that minnowy world of weeds and ditches,
When the herons floated high over the white houses,
And the little crabs slipped into silvery craters.
When the sun for me glinted the sides of a sand grain,
And my intent stretched over the buds at their first trembling.

That air and shine: and the flicker's loud summer call:
The bearded boards in the stream and the all of apples;
The glad hen on the hill; and the trellis humming.
Death was not. I lived in a simple drowse:
Hands and hair moved through a dream of wakening blossoms.
Rain sweetened the cave and the dove still called;
The flowers leaned on themselves, the flowers in hollows;
And love, love sang toward.

5

To have the whole air!–
The light, the full sun
Coming down on the flowerheads,
The tendrils turning slowly,
A slow snail-lifting, liquescent;
To be by the rose
Rising slowly out of its bed,
Still as a child in its first loneliness;

To see cyclamen veins become clearer in early sunlight,
And mist lifting out of the brown cat-tails;
To stare into the after-light, the glitter left on the lake's surface,
When the sun has fallen behind a wooded island;
To follow the drops sliding from a lifted oar,
Held up, while the rower breathes, and the small boat drifts quietly
        shoreward;
To know that light falls and fills, often without our knowing,
As an opaque vase fills to the brim from a quick pouring,
Fills and trembles at the edge yet does not flow over,
Still holding and feeding the stem of the contained flower.

[This sequence is continued in *Praise to the End!*, Part II, and concluded
with "O, Thou Opening, O" in *The Waking*.]

### Where Knock Is Open Wide

1

A kitten can
Bitc with his feet;
Papa and Mamma
Have more teeth.

Sit and play
Under the rocker
Until the cows
All have puppies.

His ears haven't time.
Sing me a sleep-song, please.
A real hurt is soft.

Once upon a tree
I came across a time,
It wasn't even as
A ghoulie in a dream.

There was a mooly man
Who had a rubber hat
The funnier than that,–
He kept it in a can.

What's the time, papa-seed?
Everything has been twice.
My father is a fish.

2

I sing a small sing,
My uncle's away,
He's gone for always,
I don't care either.

I know who's got him,
They'll jump on his belly,
He won't be an angel,
I don't care either.

I know her noise.
Her neck has kittens.
I'll make a hole for her.
In the fire.

Winkie will yellow I sang.
Her eyes went kissing away
It was and it wasn't her there
I sang I sang all day.

3

I know it's an owl. He's making it darker.
Eat where you're at. I'm not a mouse.
Some stones are still warm.
I like soft paws.
Maybe I'm lost,
Or asleep.

A worm has a mouth.
Who keeps me last?
Fish me out.
Please.

God, give me a near. I hear flowers.
A ghost can't whistle.
I know! I know!
Hello happy hands.

4

We went by the river.
Water birds went ching. Went ching.
Stepped in wet. Over stones.
One, his nose had a frog,
But he slipped out.

I was sad for a fish.
Don't hit him on the boat, I said.
Look at him puff. He's trying to talk.
Papa threw him back.

Bullheads have whiskers.
And they bite.

He watered the roses.
His thumb had a rainbow.
The stems said, Thank you.
Dark came early.

That was before. I fell! I fell!
The worm has moved away.
My tears are tired.

Nowhere is out. I saw the cold.
Went to visit the wind. Where the birds die.
How high is have?
I'll be a bite. You be a wink.
Sing the snake to sleep.

5

Kisses come back,
I said to Papa;
He was all whitey bones
And skin like paper.

God's somewhere else,
I said to Mamma.
The evening came
A long long time.

I'm somebody else now.
Don't tell my hands.
Have I come to always? Not yet.
One father is enough.

Maybe God has a house.
But not here.

*A Walk in Late Summer*

1

A gull rides on the ripples of a dream,
White upon white, slow-settling on a stone;
Across my lawn the soft-backed creatures come;
In the weak light they wander, each alone.
Bring me the meek, for I would know their ways;
I am a connoisseur of midnight eyes.
The small! The small! I hear them singing clear
On the long banks, in the soft summer air.

2

What is there for the soul to understand?
The slack face of the dismal pure inane?
The wind dies down; my will dies with the wind,

God's in that stone, or I am not a man!
Body and soul transcend appearances
Before the caving-in of all that is;
I'm dying piecemeal, fervent in decay;
My moments linger–that's eternity.

3

A late rose ravages the casual eye,
A blaze of being on a central stem.
It lies upon us to undo the lie
Of living merely in the realm of time.
Existence moves toward a certain end–
A thing all earthly lovers understand.
That dove's elaborate way of coming near
Reminds me I am dying with the year.

4

A tree arises on a central plain—
It is no trick of change or chance of light.
A tree all out of shape from wind and rain,
A tree thinned by the wind obscures my sight.
The long day dies; I walked the woods alone;
Beyond the ridge two wood thrush sing as one.
Being delights in being, and in time.
The evening wraps me, steady as a flame.

### The Far Field

1

I dream of journeys repeatedly:
Of flying like a bat deep into a narrowing tunnel,
Of driving alone, without luggage, out a long peninsula,
The road lined with snow-laden second growth,
A fine dry snow ticking the windshield,
Alternate snow and sleet, no on-coming traffic,

And no lights behind, in the blurred side-mirror,
The road changing from glazed tarface to a rubble of stone,
Ending at last in a hopeless sand-rut,
Where the car stalls,
Churning in a snowdrift
Until the headlights darken.

2

At the field's end, in the corner missed by the mower,
Where the turf drops off into a grass-hidden culvert,
Haunt of the cat-bird, nesting-place of the field-mouse,
Not too far away from the ever-changing flower-dump,
Among the tin cans, tires, rusted pipes, broken machinery,—
One learned of the eternal;
And in the shrunken face of a dead rat, eaten by rain and ground-
    beetles
(I found it lying among the rubble of an old coal bin)
And the tom-cat, caught near the pheasant-run,
Its entrails strewn over the half-grown flowers,
Blasted to death by the night watchman.

I suffered for birds, for young rabbits caught in the mower,
My grief was not excessive.
For to come upon warblers in early May
Was to forget time and death:
How they filled the oriole's elm, a twittering restless cloud, all one
    morning,
And I watched and watched till my eyes blurred from the bird
    shapes,—
Cape May, Blackburnian, Cerulean,—
Moving, elusive as fish, fearless,
Hanging, bunched like young fruit, bending the end branches,
Still for a moment,
Then pitching away in half-flight,
Lighter than finches,
While the wrens bickered and sang in the half-green hedgerows,
And the flicker drummed from his dead tree in the chicken-yard.

–Or to lie naked in sand,
In the silted shallows of a slow river,
Fingering a shell,
Thinking:
Once I was something like this, mindless,
Or perhaps with another mind, less peculiar;
Or to sink down to the hips in a mossy quagmire;
Or, with skinny knees, to sit astride a wet log,
Believing:
I'll return again,
As a snake or a raucous bird,
Or, with luck, as a lion.

I learned not to fear infinity,
The far field, the windy cliffs of forever,
The dying of time in the white light of tomorrow,
The wheel turning away from itself,
The sprawl of the wave,
The on-coming water.

3

The river turns on itself,
The tree retreats into its own shadow.
I feel a weightless change, a moving forward
As of water quickening before a narrowing channel
When banks converge, and the wide river whitens;
Or when two rivers combine, the blue glacial torrent
And the yellowish-green from the mountainy upland,–
At first a swift rippling between rocks,
Then a long running over flat stones
Before descending to the alluvial plain,
To the clay banks, and the wild grapes hanging from the elmtrees.
The slightly trembling water
Dropping a fine yellow silt where the sun stays;
And the crabs bask near the edge,
The weedy edge, alive with small snakes and bloodsuckers,–
I have come to a still, but not a deep center,

A point outside the glittering current;
My eyes stare at the bottom of a river,
At the irregular stones, iridescent sandgrains,
My mind moves in more than one place,
In a country half-land, half-water.

I am renewed by death, thought of my death,
The dry scent of a dying garden in September,
The wind fanning the ash of a low fire.
What I love is near at hand,
Always, in earth and air.

4

The lost self changes,
Turning toward the sea,
A sea-shape turning around,–
An old man with his feet before the fire,
In robes of green, in garments of adieu.

A man faced with his own immensity
Wakes all the waves, all their loose wandering fire.
The murmur of the absolute, the why
Of being born fails on his naked ears.
His spirit moves like monumental wind
That gentles on a sunny blue plateau.
He is the end of things, the final man.

All finite things reveal infinitude:
The mountain with its singular bright shade
Like the blue shine on freshly frozen snow,
The after-light upon ice-burdened pines;
Odor of basswood on a mountain-slope,
A scent beloved of bees;
Silence of water above a sunken tree:
The pure serene of memory in one man,–
A ripple widening from a single stone
Winding around the waters of the world.

# PAUL GOODMAN [1911-1972]

Paul Goodman was born in New York City. He received a B.A. from the City College in New York and a Ph.D. from the University of Chicago. In the following years, he taught at the University of Chicago, New York University, Black Mountain College, Sarah Lawrence College, and the universities of Wisconsin and Hawaii. Despite his formidable gifts as a poet, Goodman is primarily known for his works of social criticism. In 1960, his *Growing Up Absurd*, a study of the plight of urban youth, made him famous. Also notable is his *Utopian Essays & Practical Proposals* (1962) and the linguistic study *Speaking and Language: Defense of Poetry* (1972). There is a lyrical and spontaneous quality to much of Goodman's verse. His *Collected Poems*, edited by Taylor Stoehr, was published by Random House in 1974.

### For My Birthday, 1939

I walking on my birthday met a young
Enterprise, Hope and Animal Spirits' boy,
and I had the crazy thought again to try.
He was like a banjo, bright and high-strung
and jazzy with, no doubt, a wicked tongue,
and so I fell in step with him and "Why
do you avoid me? don't you like to play?"
I hinted and my heart was hammering.
"You're middle-aged!" "Only twenty-eight.
There are lots of older poets, Enterprise."
"But you have given hostages to fate,
that sky-blue car, your cat, your daughter, these
multiply accidents you don't create,
collisions, wild dogs, and disease."

In the Universe of Correspondences
–my longing and the things, my longing and
my reaching, my longing and their presences–
this is the rule: where I stretch my hand,
darlings dissipate to absences,
my call is terrible and my command
exacts unerringly their disobedience,
and like Lot's wife where I stand, I stand.
Except my gentle Peace–I do not seek–
comes freely to me. Quietly we speak.
She says, "You pious man, you pay your debt
to the Creator of the heavens and the earth."
And I reply, "A little longer yet
attending to these things of little worth."


### For Sally, with a Piano

This old piano with a sweeter treble
and a strong deep voice to you we brothers give;
no longer inconsolably grieve,
Sally, that Scarlatti's brilliant ripple

and Haydn's *Variations* are unplayable.
This quaint old box of strings will not deceive
your touch but courteously come alive,
the action is brand new and serviceable.

I came upon you weeping in despair
seated at a bad piano in
the accidents of life. God knows how far
beyond me each day is, and physical pain
doubles my bafflement; and yet we in-
novate this detail and that detail repair.


### Reading Adonais

Sternly my eyebrows meet as murmuring
the measured verses I read Shelley's lust
to die ill-hidden in this rapturous
paean to eternity the beckoning
Hesperus on the water. How they sting,
the sentences that life holds out to us
nothing, and never did, though I discuss
my memories back to the early spring,
but disappointed days, which as my grim
autumn sets in have at last downed me.
                                                                So
about the other English poet dead
in this dead poet's book whose stanzas glow
incandescent with his even hymn
to blinding light before he sailed, I read.


### The Lordly Hudson

"Driver, what stream is it?" I asked, well knowing
it was our lordly Hudson hardly flowing,
"It is our lordly Hudson hardly flowing,"
he said, "under the green-grown cliffs."

Be still, heart! no one needs your passionate
suffrage to select this glory,
this is our lordly Hudson hardly flowing
under the green-grown cliffs.

"Driver! has this a peer in Europe or the East?"
"No no!" he said. Home! home!
be quiet, heart! this is our lordly Hudson
and has no peer in Europe or the East,

this is our lordly Hudson hardly flowing
under the green-grown cliffs
and has no peer in Europe or the East.
Be quiet, heart! home! home!


*Saint Cecilia's Day, 1941*

"Admit that it means something!"
–Beethoven, to Goethe

They all looked dead with tingling ears,
close-eyed and open-mouthed, or open-eyed
with mouths closed, their limbs involuntary.
The voices of the instruments harmonized
the ages and sexes of humanity
squeals of little children and the clear
warbling of women and sonorous males.
You would not think the world was at war.
Lastly silence, which is quiet
only after music or when the passions
are finished.
                    The flood of life returned
into our brains and we were separate,
into our legs we rose and came outside.
But it was the holiday of Saint Harmony
and after saying nothing for awhile
drinking our drinks we said in praise of music:

I.

Lothario said. "Heaven and hell, I was
so sensitive sometimes a major triad
of wooden oboes drilled me like a toothache,
they added fourths and my head split. The chaos
of mixed timbres, say the whine of strings
with a piano, oh it separated
my organism into protozoa,
a horn croaked and they curled their feet and died.
Naturally, when I was in school
they called me tone-deaf and told me not to sing.
What the teacher used to call a unison
was a chasm you could drop a desk and chair in.
"If in this agony I inwardly
would close my ears as I can,
as others close their nostrils against a stink,
then could I hear the music of the spheres.
For know that the creator of the heavens
standing on Canto Fermo forth first breathed
the solemn vibration of the sun
*alla breve* and filled it out with planets
and passing notes of comets with long tails.
These tones are sustained. Millennia
elapse to the measure, and there is no
cadence yet—the cadence is to come.
The ear hears nothing of it, but the body
flows in tides.
            "I can't," he bitterly
whispered, "hear that music any more.
But I am wiser than I was. To noises!
noises of fire, void, and violence
and interminable continuity
God listens patiently. A stretto trill
in all the voices. Surely the frame
is strong or would by now have cracked, and man
man have fragmented into fractional
intervals and evaporated—"

He paused;
for everywhere the Man was waging war
but had not yet dropped the first atom bomb.

"At other times, as mildly tonight,
I hear such tones: *'who listens to these tones*
*will never know sorrow more.'"*
                                    "Why do you say it
with death in your eyes if it is so?"
"No. It is so. It is really so."


## II.


The architect began more merrily.
"You know Amphion built Thebes with a song,
by harmony on the Boeotian plain.
Now I have had the happy thought of him
standing in a rowboat on the Hudson
while all the fishes look with open mouths
*untuning* with a supersonic lyre
a thing or two or three or four or five.

"His nail is screeching on the wire strings
and the tip-top of the Empire State Building
conceived as a mooring-mast for Zeppelins
falls like they. The gilt Prometheus
sinks in the pond. Columbia's South Hall
—now there's a building where you could not change
a line without improving the proportions—
he ruins with a flourish, all the fishes
joyfully leap out of the water to see.

"Now Central Park, it once was wild and gay
with bushes for the privacy of love
before another Moses gave it laws
and subsidized the hotels—therefore praise,
you fairies and sailorboys and little whores,
Amphion's name forevermore! he doused
the officious lights, but left the silent moon.

He rubbed the prude off Fiorello's face,
Thomas Dewey he left half a mustache.
My friends! let me have another drink.
"With a large arm Amphion sweeps the strings!
The modulus, the modulus take not
from iron girders or a two-by-four,
take it from the grandeur of a man
standard of doorways. Let the outside in
and inside out, so the space can move;
measure it, so the space can dance.
What is proportion? Lay out twos and threes
on the horizontal for the walking, skipping,
instantaneously leaping eyes,
and where we see perspectively draw in
irrational diagonals. All masses
want finally to rest, do not thwart them;
but passion and pleasure, they are curves that wander,
let them soar—
                    "Where was I?" he asked
and then like Palinurus drowsed and drowned.

### III.

I said, "I pass. After that, I pass.
However, let me ask Herman a question:
that music that you played tonight,
what does that music mean?

"Say, have you ever watched him, bow in hand,
for the florid Concert in the Key of D?
—suddenly the symphony's alive
without the solo, all its veiny tendrils
ramifying into foliage
and rosebuds without Herman! he must wait.
'There goes my tune,' he mutters in his mustache,
'if I'd a known it I'd a stood in bed.'
His bow hangs down forgotten. Finally
he drops the fiddle from his chin and listens.

'This is so strong and sweet that I could listen
to only this.' No, no, now Herman play!
it's time.
   "We know his phrases, how they pause
in the air, like flowers, in still air, in June."
I turned to him.

IV.

   But in his changing eyes
were many thoughts and he said in a voice of pain
—so it sounded, but he is hard to read—
"The first years that I played the Quartet
in C-Sharp Minor that we played tonight
—and who knows these tones will know no sorrow more—
I thought, This is just absent-mindedness,
heat lightning, a jig for a carousel;
along with the great heart the mind got tired,
and that is what's written in the score.

"I bent my head. His faults also were songs.
Jokes are the poetry of desperation.
Lapses are the poetry of fatigue.
Heat lightning is a memory of power.
Son, whatever is lost is the meaning of music
and agony is written in the score.
When I play it, if I sometimes weep
my tears are not for only Beethoven."

"Who knows these tones," Lothario assured him,
"will never know sorrow more."
      "After a while
I myself played it better, and I thought:
Here's an ingenious machine for Joy,
to force the joy to be where no joy is.
Every part of it is put together
with the cunning of a man who knew himself
and therefore knew how to distract himself.
Explaining it, Beethoven quickly said,

'It's made of what I picked up here and there.'
Yes, he had lots of notebooks to ransack
in winter like a squirrel. He kept busy.
I too kept busy, twenty seven times
around the world, a virtuoso fiddler!

"It happened one day that I ceased to think
and listened–as he listened who was deaf–
where beyond these tones opens the silent world,
and suddenly, like a sick memory
that strikes a patient and the veil is raised,
I saw again the horrifying scene
when Goethe burst in tears and Beethoven
leapt from the piano where he was improvising
and shook him and cried out, 'Admit! admit!
admit! admit! admit that it means something!'

*Something* is there. Something *must* be there.

and what if it's nothing?

                              "I'll play these tones no more!
I felt the weakness creep into my hand
and with an awful sound the G-string broke."

"No, Herman, but you didn't play at all."

"I didn't hold a bow for seven years."

"Ah! ah, I thought that it was longer."

"I didn't try each impasse to the end
but only till I got the idea."

"What! have you tried them all?" I cried in envy.
"Yes."
            *Yes!?* what was this simple Yes?
the appetite of man is infinite.
But I held my peace.

He said, "Who knows these tones
will know no sorrow more. If you would know,
if you would know these tones!–
a pleasing truth is written in the score,
all that is best is easiest.
Your ordinary mind, *that* is the Way!
when you feel sleepy sleep, etcetera,
if you are dying whimper.
Who *knows* these tones will never know sorrow more."


### General Washington

Hot-headed patriots, many of them bigoted
and avaricious narrow tradesmen
–it was a contradiction, petty bourgeois
impetuously taking the big risks
of war with stingy measures. Much they did
who can praise? and yet they did one deed
wise beyond praise as if inspired
by an uncanny forethought Congress chose
Washington. Not a New Englander
but from a class and country that bred soldiers,
a character in history unique
to be among stubborn freemen
Commander-in-Chief for seven awful years,
and then go home.

He was prudent to a fault in the short run.
But falling back across New York and Jersey
he guarded there would be a longer run
and did not wait too long, but fell on Trenton.

Diffident he was, like one who thinks
of everything where much must be in doubt,
and so he listened too much to his staff
when his own judgment was superior;
yet–sharing blunders he made officers
for the war that had to drag in any case

till the King gave up at his slow-witted speed.

And isn't it beautiful and noteworthy
how youngsters, the adventurous and brilliant,
the Hamiltons and Lafayettes, adored him
(I choose the word with care) not servilely?
He must have been like a father to them
so that they also grew into the future.
So we can guess his heartsick shock
come to West Point and Arnold wasn't there.
"My mind misgave me," said the General,
"I had no idea of the real cause,"
although methodically he had observed
all the small signs, but he was not suspicious.
Then Washington's dismay it was, I think,
bursting into the tears he never shed,
that scalded André, whom he wouldn't yield
even a military death but hanged him
from a gallows. (Gentlemen of those times
set store upon the style, though dead is dead.)
He was merciless, not like himself.
When Lee fell back for no good reason at Monmouth,
he "swore until the leaves shook on the trees"
and held the line and rallied, for the men
were awestruck. Mostly, but, he was unmoved
by a mischance and did the best he could,
except it was different before Yorktown!
"I am distressed beyond expression!"
he fretted like a child as he flew south,
and laid his careful plans, the time he scented,
but would not own it yet, the victory.
By this time he was flexible like lightning
that leaps the high potential.
       Washington's
integrity in all the other things,
money, rank, or the nice points of honor
–among the graspers in and out of Congress
and in the army (and the King of England
still thought to make George Washington a duke!

but not hereditary! said the King)
–was so Olympian that he was spared
intrigues, they dissipated when he looked.

Nor did he threaten once–this is remarkable!–
to quit, as a weapon, though he was
sometimes in despair
and truly might, though not a praying man,
have knelt in the snow, as in the picture.

So might a poet, avid to praise,
avid to praise loud but hard to please,
praise Washington and call the Congress wise.
And still he looms there in the dubious past
real. He does not need interpretation.
Transparent in his virtues and his limits,
not greatly superior in any crisis,
superior enough in every crisis,
a Commander-in-Chief! it is a man whose peers
or abler men in this and that respect,
do not need to make allowances for him
but confidently speak and will be heard.
For war is senseless, its suffering is senseless,
but it is demonic, it is mankind gone mad,
and lucky is the people if its leaders
warrant ordinary admiration
as noble honest men who are not fools.

Such, he seemed like a god to wise old tired
Europe, where we meet, with pleased surprise,
our Washington on little village squares.
It's reasonable that his statue is there.

## ELIZABETH BISHOP   [1911-1979]

Elizabeth Bishop was born in Worcester, Massachusetts. Her father died when she was only eight months old; when she was five, her mother was committed to a mental institution, and Elizabeth never saw her again. Her childhood was spent with relatives in New England and Nova Scotia. She graduated from Vassar College in 1934, and, subsequently, lived in New York City, Key West, and Brazil (where she remained for sixteen years). Her first book of poetry, *North & South*, was published in 1946; nine years later, it was issued jointly with *A Cold Spring*, and the volume was awarded a Pulitzer Prize. Her *Complete Poems* (1969) won the National Book Award, and in 1976 she became the first woman and the first American to receive the Books Abroad Neustadt International for Literature Prize. In her later years, she taught creative writing at Harvard University.

## The Map

Land lies in water; it is shadowed green.
Shadows, or are they shallows, at its edges
showing the line of long sea-weeded ledges
where weeds hang to the simple blue from green.
Or does the land lean down to lift the sea from under,
drawing it unperturbed around itself?
Along the fine tan sandy shelf
is the land tugging at the sea from under?

The shadow of Newfoundland lies flat and still.
Labrador's yellow, where the moony Eskimo
has oiled it. We can stroke these lovely bays,
under a glass as if they were expected to blossom,
or as if to provide a clean cage for invisible fish.
The names of seashore towns run out to sea,
the names of cities cross the neighboring mountains
–the printer here experiencing the same excitement
as when emotion too far exceeds its cause.
These peninsulas take the water between thumb and finger
like women feeling for the smoothness of yard-goods.

Mapped waters are more quiet than the land is,
lending the land their waves' own conformation:
and Norway's hare runs south in agitation,
profiles investigate the sea, where land is.
Are they assigned, or can the countries pick their colors?
–What suits the character or the native waters best.
Topography displays no favorites; North's as near as West.
More delicate than the historians' are the map-makers' colors.

## The Imaginary Iceberg

We'd rather have the iceberg than the ship,
although it meant the end of travel.
Although it stood stock-still like cloudy rock
and all the sea were moving marble.
We'd rather have the iceberg than the ship;
we'd rather own this breathing plain of snow
though the ship's sails were laid upon the sea
as the snow lies undissolved upon the water.
O solemn, floating field,
are you aware an iceberg takes repose
with you, and when it wakes may pasture on your snows?

This is a scene a sailor'd give his eyes for.
The ship's ignored. The iceberg rises
and sinks again; its glassy pinnacles
correct elliptics in the sky.
This is a scene where he who treads the boards
is artlessly rhetorical. The curtain
is light enough to rise on finest ropes
that airy twists of snow provide.
The wits of these white peaks
spar with the sun. Its weight the iceberg dares
upon a shifting stage and stands and stares.

This iceberg cuts its facets from within.
Like jewelry from a grave
it saves itself perpetually and adorns
only itself, perhaps the snows
which so surprise us lying on the sea.
Good-bye, we say, good-bye, the ship steers off
where waves give in to one another's waves
and clouds run in a warmer sky.
Icebergs behoove the soul
(both being self-made from elements least visible)
to see them so: fleshed, fair, erected indivisible.

## The Man-Moth*

Here, above,
cracks in the buildings are filled with battered moonlight.
The whole shadow of Man is only as big as his hat.
It lies at his feet like a circle for a doll to stand on,
and he makes an inverted pin, the point magnetized to the moon.
He does not see the moon; he observes only her vast properties,
feeling the queer light on his hands, neither warm nor cold,
of a temperature impossible to record in thermometers.

But when the Man-Moth
pays his rare, although occasional, visits to the surface,
the moon looks rather different to him. He emerges
from an opening under the edge of one of the sidewalks
and nervously begins to scale the faces of the buildings.
He thinks the moon is a small hole at the top of the sky,
proving the sky quite useless for protection.
He trembles, but must investigate as high as he can climb.

Up the façades,
his shadow dragging like a photographer's cloth behind him,
he climbs fearfully, thinking that this time he will manage
to push his small head through that round clean opening
and be forced through, as from a tube, in black scrolls on the light.
(Man, standing below him, has no such illusions.)
But what the Man-Moth fears most he must do, although
he fails, of course, and falls back scared but quite unhurt.

Then he returns
to the pale subways of cement he calls his home. He flits,
he flutters, and cannot get aboard the silent trains
fast enough to suit him. The doors close swiftly.
The Man-Moth always seats himself facing the wrong way
and the train starts at once at its full, terrible speed,
without a shift in gears or a gradation of any sort.
He cannot tell the rate at which he travels backwards.

* *Newspaper misprint for "mammoth."*

Each night he must
be carried through artificial tunnels and dream recurrent dreams.
Just as the ties recur beneath his train, these underlie
his rushing brain. He does not dare look out the window,
for the third rail, the unbroken draught of poison,
runs there beside him. He regards it as a disease
he has inherited the susceptibility to. He has to keep
his hands in his pockets, as others must wear mufflers.

If you catch him,
hold up a flashlight to his eye. It's all dark pupil,
an entire night itself, whose haired horizon tightens
as he stares back, and closes up the eye. Then from the lids
one tear, his only possession, like the bee's sting, slips.
Slyly he palms it, and if you're not paying attention
he'll swallow it. However, if you watch, he'll hand it over,
cool as from underground springs and pure enough to drink.

### The Monument

Now can you see the monument? It is of wood
built somewhat like a box. No. Built
like several boxes in descending sizes
one above the other.
Each is turned half-way round so that
its corners point toward the sides
of the one below and the angles alternate.
Then on the topmost cube is set
a sort of fleur-de-lys of weathered wood,
long petals of board, pierced with odd holes,
four-sided, stiff, ecclesiastical.
From it four thin, warped poles spring out,
(slanted like fishing-poles or flag-poles)
and from them jig-saw work hangs down,
four lines of vaguely whittled ornament
over the edges of the boxes
to the ground.

The monument is one-third set against
a sea; two-thirds against a sky.
The view is geared
(that is, the view's perspective)
so low there is no "far away,"
and we are far away within the view.
A sea of narrow, horizontal boards
lies out behind our lonely monument,
its long grains alternating right and left
like floor-boards–spotted, swarming-still,
and motionless. A sky runs parallel,
and it is palings, coarser than the sea's:
splintery sunlight and long-fibred clouds.
"Why does that strange sea make no sound?
Is it because we're far away?
Where are we? Are we in Asia Minor,
or in Mongolia?"
                    An ancient promontory,
an ancient principality whose artist-prince
might have wanted to build a monument
to mark a tomb or boundary, or make
a melancholy or romantic scene of it . . .
"But that queer sea looks made of wood,
half-shining, like a driftwood sea.
And the sky looks wooden, grained with cloud.
It's like a stage-set; it is all so flat!
Those clouds are full of glistening splinters!
What is that?"
                    It is the monument.
"It's piled-up boxes,
outlined with shoddy fret-work, half-fallen off,
cracked and unpainted. It looks old."
–The strong sunlight, the wind from the sea,
all the conditions of its existence,
may have flaked off the paint, if ever it was painted,
and made it homelier than it was.
"Why did you bring me here to see it?
A temple of crates in cramped and crated scenery,
what can it prove?

I am tired of breathing this eroded air,
this dryness in which the monument is cracking."
It is an artifact
of wood. Wood holds together better
than sea or cloud or sand could by itself,
much better than real sea or sand or cloud.
It chose that way to grow and not to move.
The monument's an object, yet those decorations,
carelessly nailed, looking like nothing at all,
give it away as having life, and wishing;
wanting to be a monument, to cherish something.
The crudest scroll-work says "commemorate,"
while once each day the light goes around it
like a prowling animal,
or the rain falls on it, or the wind blows into it.
It may be solid, may be hollow.
The bones of the artist-prince may be inside
or far away on even drier soil.
But roughly but adequately it can shelter
what is within (which after all
cannot have been intended to be seen).
It is the beginning of a painting,
a piece of sculpture, or poem, or monument,
and all of wood. Watch it closely.


## Florida

The state with the prettiest name,
the state that floats in brackish water,
held together by mangrove roots
that bear while living oysters in clusters,
and when dead strew white swamps with skeletons,
dotted as if bombarded, with green hummocks
like ancient cannon-balls sprouting grass.
The state full of long S-shaped birds, blue and white,
and unseen hysterical birds who rush up the scale
every time in a tantrum.

Tanagers embarrassed by their flashiness,
and pelicans whose delight it is to clown;
who coast for fun on the strong tidal currents
in and out among the mangrove islands
and stand on the sand-bars drying their damp gold wings
on sun-lit evenings.
Enormous turtles, helpless and mild,
die and leave their barnacled shells on the beaches,
and their large white skulls with round eye-sockets
twice the size of a man's.
The palm trees clatter in the stiff breeze
like the bills of the pelicans. The tropical rain comes down
to freshen the tide-looped strings of fading shells:
Job's Tear, the Chinese Alphabet, the scarce Junonia,
parti-colored pectins and Ladies' Ears,
arranged as on a gray rag of rotted calico,
the buried Indian Princess's skirt;
with these the monotonous, endless, sagging coast-line
is delicately ornamented.

Thirty or more buzzards are drifting down, down, down,
over something they have spotted in the swamp,
in circles like stirred-up flakes of sediment
sinking through water.
Smoke from woods-fires filters fine blue solvents.
On stumps and dead trees the charring is like black velvet.
The mosquitoes
go hunting to the tune of their ferocious obbligatos.
After dark, the fireflies map the heavens in the marsh
until the moon rises.
Cold white, not bright, the moonlight is coarse-meshed,
and the careless, corrupt state is all black specks
too far apart, and ugly whites; the poorest
post-card of itself.
After dark, the pools seem to have slipped away.
The alligator, who has five distinct calls:
friendliness, love, mating, war, and a warning—
whimpers and speaks in the throat
of the Indian Princess.

## The Fish

I caught a tremendous fish
and held him beside the boat
half out of water, with my hook
fast in a corner of his mouth.
He didn't fight.
He hadn't fought at all.
He hung a grunting weight,
battered and venerable
and homely. Here and there
his brown skin hung in strips
like ancient wallpaper,
and its pattern of darker brown
was like wallpaper:
shapes like full-blown roses
stained and lost through age.
He was speckled with barnacles,
fine rosettes of lime,
and infested
with tiny white sea-lice,
and underneath two or three
rags of green weed hung down.
While his gills were breathing in
the terrible oxygen
–the frightening gills,
fresh and crisp with blood,
that can cut so badly–
I thought of the coarse white flesh
packed in like feathers,
the big bones and the little bones,
the dramatic reds and blacks
of his shiny entrails,
and the pink swim-bladder
like a big peony.
I looked into his eyes
which were far larger than mine
but shallower, and yellowed,
the irises backed and packed

with tarnished tinfoil
seen through the lenses
of old scratched isinglass.
They shifted a little, but not
to return my stare.
—It was more like the tipping
of an object toward the light.
I admired his sullen face,
the mechanism of his jaw,
and then I saw
that from his lower lip
—if you could call it a lip—
grim, wet, and weaponlike,
hung five old pieces of fish-line,
or four and a wire leader
with the swivel still attached,
with all their five big hooks
grown firmly in his mouth.
A green line, frayed at the end
where he broke it, two heavier lines,
and a fine black thread
still crimped from the strain and snap
when it broke and he got away.
Like medals with their ribbons
frayed and wavering,
a five-haired beard of wisdom
trailing from his aching jaw.
I stared and stared
and victory filled up
the little rented boat,
from the pool of bilge
where oil had spread a rainbow
around the rusted engine
to the bailer rusted orange,
the sun-cracked thwarts,
the oarlocks on their strings,
the gunnels—until everything
was rainbow, rainbow, rainbow!
And I let the fish go.

## A *Cold Spring*

For Jane Dewey, Maryland

Nothing is so beautiful as spring.—Hopkins

A cold spring:
the violet was flawed on the lawn.
For two weeks or more the trees hesitated;
the little leaves waited,
carefully indicating their characteristics.
Finally a grave green dust
settled over your big and aimless hills.
One day, in a chill white blast of sunshine,
on the side of one a calf was born.
The mother stopped lowing
and took a long time eating the after-birth,
a wretched flag,
but the calf got up promptly
and seemed inclined to feel gay.

The next day
was much warmer.
Greenish-white dogwood infiltrated the wood,
each petal burned, apparently, by a cigarette-butt;
and the blurred redbud stood
beside it, motionless, but almost more
like movement than any placeable color.
Four deer practised leaping over your fences.
The infant oak-leaves swung through the sober oak.
Song-sparrows were wound up for the summer,
and in the maple the complementary cardinal
cracked a whip, and the sleeper awoke,
stretching miles of green limbs from the south.
In his cap the lilacs whitened,
then one day they fell like snow.
Now, in the evening,
a new moon comes.
The hills grow softer. Tufts of long grass show

where each cow-flop lies.
The bull-frogs are sounding,
slack strings plucked by heavy thumbs.
Beneath the light, against your white front door,
the smallest moths, like Chinese fans,
flatten themselves, silver and silver-gilt
over pale yellow, orange, or gray.
Now, from the thick grass, the fireflies
begin to rise:
up, then down, then up again:
lit on the ascending flight,
drifting simultaneously to the same height,
–exactly like the bubbles in champagne.
–Later on they rise much higher.
And your shadowy pastures will be able to offer
these particular glowing tributes
every evening now throughout the summer.


## Questions of Travel

There are too many waterfalls here; the crowded streams
hurry too rapidly down to the sea,
and the pressure of so many clouds on the mountaintops
makes them spill over the sides in soft slow-motion,
turning to waterfalls under our very eyes.
–For if those streaks, those mile-long, shiny, tearstains,
aren't waterfalls yet,
in a quick age or so, as ages go here,
they probably will be.
But if the streams and clouds keep travelling, travelling,
the mountains look like the hulls of capsized ships,
slime-hung and barnacled.

Think of the long trip home.
Should we have stayed at home and thought of here?
Where should we be today?
Is it right to be watching strangers in a play
in this strangest of theatres?

What childishness is it that while there's a breath of life
in our bodies, we are determined to rush
to see the sun the other way around?
The tiniest green hummingbird in the world?
To stare at some inexplicable old stonework,
inexplicable and impenetrable,
at any view,
instantly seen and always, always delightful?
Oh, must we dream our dreams
and have them, too?
And have we room
for one more folded sunset, still quite warm?

But surely it would have been a pity
not to have seen the trees along this road,
really exaggerated in their beauty,
not to have seen them gesturing
like noble pantomimists, robed in pink.
—Not to have had to stop for gas and heard
the sad, two-noted, wooden tune
of disparate wooden clogs
carelessly clacking over
a grease-stained filling-station floor.
(In another country the clogs would all be tested.
Each pair there would have identical pitch.)
—A pity not to have heard
the other, less primitive music of the fat brown bird
who sings above the broken gasoline pump
in a bamboo church of Jesuit baroque:
three towers, five silver crosses.
—Yes, a pity not to have pondered,
blurr'dly and inconclusively,
on what connection can exist for centuries
between the crudest wooden footwear
and, careful and finicky,
the whittled fantasies of wooden cages.
—Never to have studied history in
the weak calligraphy of songbirds' cages.

–And never to have had to listen to rain
so much like politicians' speeches:
two hours of unrelenting oratory
and then a sudden golden silence
in which the traveller takes a notebook, writes:

*"Is it lack of imagination that makes us come
to imagined places, not just stay at home?
Or could Pascal have been not entirely right
about just sitting quietly in one's room?*

*Continent, city, country, society:
the choice is never wide and never free.
And here, or there . . . No. Should we have stayed at home,
wherever that may be?"*

## JOSEPHINE MILES   [Born 1911]

Josephine Miles was born in Chicago, Illinois, and moved with her family to California when she was five years old. Miles received her B.A. at the University of California at Los Angeles and then did graduate work at Berkeley, where she went on to teach for nearly forty years. She published ten volumes of verse, among them *Lines at Intersection* (1939), *Poems on Several Occasions* (1941), *Local Measures* (1946), and, most recently, *Coming to Terms* (1979). Also a well-known critic, Miles produced several textbooks as well as studies on poetry and poetics. During her career, Miles was much-honored, receiving the Shelley Memorial Award, the National Institute of Arts and Letters Award for poetry, and the Modern Language Association's James Russell Lowell Prize. Her poems are sparse and colloquial; she wrote that it was her aim to reveal the "truths" which underlie "all appearances," the "joy in simplicity," and the "large ideas in small talk."

### Herald

Delivers papers to the doors of sleep,
Tosses up news upon the shores of sleep
In the day's damp, in the street's swamp wades deep
And is himself the boy drowned, drowned with sleep.

Crosses to the corner with the lamp
Already dark, even asleep with the lamp,
Treads in the wet grass, wares, leaps as in swamp
The gutters dark with darkening of the lamp.

Hears only the thud and thud against the doors
Of the news falling asleep against the doors,
The slip and drip of mist on the two shores,
Sees without light or sight the coasts of doors.

Sees at a door a light, Herald, Sir?
Wakes to the whistle and light, Herald, Sir?
To the latch lifted and the face's blur
Wakes; wakes coin, day, greeting, Herald, Sir.

### Seer

The psychic metaphysician sat tight in the white
Shine of the rocks outside Riverside,
It was like living in a world of mirrors
The left-hand rocks and leaves so took the light,
The left of cornflakes in the kitchenette
So took the light.

Is it wind or is it a new year, asked the psychic metaphysician
Resting his hand upon the parlor chair, and the flare
Of answers long lying in that dust dazzled him,
The left-hand cups and mirrors so took the light,
It was like living in a world of answers
The hand so took the light.

I shall be prodigal with thine information
The psychic metaphysician knelt and spelt,
Changing fifty cents to forty on his sign,
It swung against the porch and took the light,
It was like living in a world of sight
The sign so took the light.


### Personification

She will define for you in the sunny morning
The self possessed.
Where are you going (my pretty maid)?
I'm going shopping (sir) she said.
Her foot on the brake is self possessed, and it shines,
Her hand on the wheel is self possessed, and the lines
Of lapel and brim, of seam and hem
Are self possessed.

The power of keys is hers
And self possessed.
Two bits for the parking (my pretty maid),
Here is your quarter (sir) she said,
And the quarter is self possessed, see it shine,
And the shine of the palm it lies in, and the line
Of chin and throat that lift to let you note
Them self possessed.

Her heel in the gravel lot
Is self possessed.
How long will you be (my pretty maid)?
About an hour (sir) she said.
Her face in the crowd is self possessed, and shining,
Her pause on the curb is self possessed, defining
To cars and stores and stares and the sun in the morning
The self possessed.

## Cat

Lady in the leopard skin
Has a fear of plunging in
Traffic like a muddy river,
Starting gives a little shiver.

Gears and peers and fears again
That her horn is not too plain;
Edges to curb, pauses to think
How to move upon the brink.

Go ahead, implores the tender,
Heavy-handed on the fender,
In her ears the engine sings
Yellow-eyed, the lady springs.


## Appointment in Doctor's Office

The lady put off her fur, it was so warm in the outer office,
She was pale but not because she was frightened. She was afraid.
She looked at the framed pictures, particularly one of mountains with
    sunlight,
Then she got out her glasses and read *Harper's Bazaar*
In which was a striking teaset of cream and jade.
She smoothed her gloves because she was afraid.

The lady would not look at the little boy waiting in the outer
    office,
Because he kept his hands together and did not smile.
She would not look at the one who held him,
Reminding him at intervals not to cry.
And yet thereafter she did reassuringly smile
For what was evidently a long while.

The lady sat with her little broken bone and thought about Hawaii,
Now and again stopping and taking breath.

Every chair was filled with the smoke of waiting,
The pages turning in intense parlor atmosphere,
Till when at the long long long overdue beckon she took breath
The lady was sick unto death.

### Romantic Letter

Dear Jo, Margaret has been taken
To Tehachapi prison in the green June,
In the summer that is here.
She will be a bird-in-cage,
She will have a raven rage.
The pickers in the little summer valleys
Will trade the peaches for the twenty cents,
And Margaret will lean her head and cry.
The softest prison breath will be her sigh
For the pennies they have not, for the warriors forgot,
For the cause not won or lost enough to die.
It is war she will wage in the pamphlet on the page.
Dreaming of her pickers in the still of summertime,
In the still of air of crime.
Jo, I think that I must write this all,
I will do a ballad of grief
And of loss, but of rising
And of Margaret, what she said.
I will give up Guinevere in the play I wrote you of,
After all, she is dead.
There is Margaret instead, and the front of criminal
Syndicalism.    Beth, with love.

### Views to See Clayton From

His brother's wife can't stand Clayton.
She's a nurse, neat and a hard worker,
And what's in Don of the radical's in him worse
And scares her more.

Don, the disk in him can be worn like leather,
She saves his life over and over
And gives it prize, polish, so they fit
Like hand in glove.

But then here's Clayton lurking about his parent's home
Looking for mischief, and a hand on his sleeve
Makes him jump. Leave him alone,
He's more trouble than we want in this world.

His father says that as a small boy
Clayton had more gumption than anyone in the family.
Nobody so quick to jump off a thirty-foot board
Into the deepest water, didn't know the name of danger.

But along about the age of discretion he must have picked some up.
Anyway from then on he always hesitated
Before he plunged off into those risks of his,
But always plunged off, coming back hurt, that's Clayton now.

His mother softly says, Clay could be a real leader.
Somewhere, how could I tell, he took not to.
He was the one with ideas, grew the garden
With the green thumb, teased the girls.
What a tease he was, softly his mother,
And still is, for that matter.

Don remembers old Clay when 69 Squadron
Flew wing to wing, given three inches
Either way the whole thing would collide,
It was his hand held those inches spaced between them,
And what a bringer, when he got off that cloud.

He was always a smart boy, Aunt Martha,
Quick, eager, couldn't put anything over on Clay.
Answering every time he got the teacher's eye,
Opinionated, but the smart are often that way.

Even cynical, you might say. How does it happen
The bright turn sour on us? It's hard to find
Of our chief leaders today any who
Showed real promise when they were young.

Damn you, Clayton, Uncle Henry says,
You're so restless, you break up everybody else's well-
    earned rest.
Career down the highway, you're apt to hit somebody.
And what will we do then with the insurance money?

Damn you, Clayton, Uncle Henry says,
Your father and I have worked for maybe forty years now
To get a steady place to put our feet on,
To put your childish feet.

When they were all sitting around in the living room
I was there too, but I didn't think I should say very much,
So I listened. How their souls rose in their mouths
To shouts almost, they were so implicated.

Go–don't–why–oh why–I always said–
You never did–not possible–impossible–
Possible–oh Clay–never–oh Clay–
He could ride them, that boy.

So I read the *S.F. Chronicle* as if I were reading.
And by and by he got up and came over and took it away.
And said, don't you care?
And I said, yes I do. But I did not get into the argument.


### Cloud

Strontium 90 is slowly falling out
From the great heights of the stratosphere.
It settles
On leaves, on housetops, on ourselves

When we stand out under the open sky.
It settles down

In the grass which cows mull into their milk,
Which children gulp into their skeletons.
How much of the stuff is now in the skies?
A good deal is up there.
It drifts and settles out,
Half of it in about twenty-four years.

In my wristbone turns up Strontium 90 a-crumble
In your set jaw, its lag.
The mortal dust we have knelt in the dust to
Rises at the horizon, so that we move
Drawing out of the mire and blowing
Clouds of the mire ahead of us as we go.


## Gypsy

The entire country is overrun with private property, the gypsy
    king said.
    I don't know if this is true,
    I believe in the gypsy kingship though.

    The lost tribes of my own nation
    Rove and rove.
    In red and yellow rough and silent move.

    I believe
    The majesty pot mending, coppersmith
    On the hundred highways, nothing to do with.

    And black eyes, black I never saw,
    Searching out the pocket lines of cloth,
    The face lines and the furrows of belief.

    It's a curious fact, Stephan, King, if you are made to doubt
    Aegyptian vision on the Jersey shore.
    Property's private as ever, ever.

### Tourists

Genealogists, geologists, and experts in falconry
Walked over the green and stony island and approved it,
Looked in the face its people and passed by them
As a rock unprocessed.

Jotted down traces of races, croppings, and the brooded bird,
The eyries of a scandic shift to believe,
But more closely what to name ancestral and to make
What plunge in the feathered spot.

Lifted on highways and at club festivals,
The host genealogists, geologists, and falconers making them
    welcome,
Eyes to the host eyes, and pressed past them
To the height where the hood be lifted for work.

### Lucifer Alone

One rat across the floor and quick to floor's a breeze,
But two a whisper of a human tongue.
One is a breath, two voice;
And one a dream, but more are dreamed too long.

Two are the portent which we may believe at length,
And two the tribe we recognize as true.
Two are the total, *they* saying and *they* saying,
So we must ponder what we are to do.

For every scuttle of motion in the corner of the eye
Some thought of thought is asked in us indeed,
But of two, more: there we have likeness moving,
And there knowledge therefore, and therefore creed.

## Headless

The man with no ears
Overhears
People talking in the park and lobby.
He is upset,
Their private ramblings concern him,
Do not let him forget
He has no ears.

What about the whole head then—
Placed either side,
Those fine organs of discrimination
Clean to the breeze—
Is it not possible such a head will hear
Just that which is spoken
And no more?

Rather, by often chance,
The delicate receivers
Bring to the brain such overtones of remorse
The whole head must operate like a blind man
Deaf and mute
Decline
To all or nothing.

And the choice
Nagging past bell to book or bark to voice
Past no to yes
Past yes to irony
Holds him the head up till its listening spirit
Wishes the hearing
Headless of itself.

*Ten Dreamers in a Motel*

1

Some people said the cabin
Wouldn't hold us two,
Two hundred and forty pounds,
Two hundred and twenty-two.

But note wherever we moved
Back or face to face
Outside the windows flew
Hundreds of butterflies.

So that within our walls,
Walls that denied us well,
Glimmered the wing that tells
All things are possible.

To elephant and elephant
Stalking exact apart,
The centennial memory
Of a light heart.

2

At this dinner I was telling you about
Next door to this motel
Was your pal your host,
And me, and a mother, daughter
Come to greet you back, how they loved you.

She for the past as if a bowl of carnations
Sat with the chicken;
She for the chicken;
He for the silverware.

The lines of life which moved between you
Like toy tramcars

Were also like toy speedsters
Building up speed.
An electric party.

Except, between us, you
And me met to greet you back,
Was absence still.
A freedom free enough to kill.

3

One day we started out
To pick up driftwood. I was interested
In a housing project there, I had heard a lecture
Illuminating the beach like lightning.
It was my concern
To raise on the shingle rows of boards
On which the great foundations could be built.

Rather, I found the shanties were up already,
And indeed down already, every one
Empty to the tide as if just then
They had been lived in but would live no more.
I turned round.
If I had been looking south I looked north
East west I turned.

4

On which of the many hills
Of suburbs out beyond the State Fair on Saturday morning
Did we pasture our goats?
Up down over the Marguerite Street district
We saw the angel ladders behind before us
But not that field in which our thoughts were bound.

Conceive if you can the animal desolation
Which besieged us on all sides other districts than our own.

We were, myself and self, not enough to ensure
Any comfort of company, but one who will say
So it is, and not let me deny, say
Let us go back by the municipal railway.

### 5

Carombed out of town in a comedy-chase fashion,
Police oblique to our path, and statues
Wheeled over, through Harlem, and all more wasteful as we went,
And ended up at this tourist cabin,
Its outlook, so it was said, restful.

Went to the window,
Pushed aside the curtains and there saw
That countryside we longed for: rocks,
Steep slopes of rocks, rubble and rusk of rocks.
What is it? and you said, *moraine*.

### 6

When we came back all the underpasses were flooded,
Highway 40 blocked off
And six inches of water at the supermarket.
So it was necessary to go round by the byroads.

So it was that we came to our street from a different view,
Saw our neighborhood from aside and below,
Stacked up the hill our houses in their shrub,
Their windows empty as an evening sky.

And so it was we saw that they dwelt without us,
Endured merrily as bastions against our presence,
Persons of note and self in the rainy evening,
Lampless and starless.

### 7

I saw a field of folk in fit array,
A circus field, or fair,
A tumbler tin-twister and auto-court carnival
Brought for the day.

Among which I went, larking and singing,
Crowding and wandering, till
Where was I? everybody wandered
While I stood still, longing

To find myself out, there to find,
And in relief
I felt at my shoulder, straight beside me,
Father or friend.

But it was not, but a strange
Present person who stood,
To whom that field fair and carnival
And I, he said, belonged.

### 8

I went to consult a psychiatrist on this morning,
A nervous woman, whose curly-headed four-year-old child
Played in the room, sitting staunchly
On a great medical scales.

I defended myself thus. It looks as if
All this weariness came from too much work,
But rather I think it a problem of person,
Friend or foe, fortune of parent or pardon.

The nervous psychiatrist ran her hand through her hair
And glanced at her watch. Have you taken a trip lately,
It would do you good, and take your mother with you,
She needs it more than you do.

Then I laughed to hear my own prescription
Given to myself with such good humor
In the gray weariness. But then she said also,
Take with you also my curly-headed four-year-old child.

9

I said to my iron class, I am desperate, desperate,
You must learn and you will not.
Each by each I looked to into the light and said
You are fast in darkness.

Each to each I said I am desperate, desperate.
Then one rose from his seat and sat beside me,
Touching my hand and saying, out of his daylight,
Do not despair.

10

Midway stayed at a court between there and here
Where woodsmoke rose up straight into the sky,
Cabin by cabin the suppers cooking
Far as the eye could see, the courts unfolding
Durable darkness.

It was the tent and citadel of the many stars,
It was the rampart of the loud highway
And we slept there, waking
Into the thunder and silence of the unfolding
Durable journey.

## KENNETH PATCHEN  [Born 1911]

Kenneth Patchen was born in Niles, Ohio, to parents of Scottish, English, and French descent. When he was seventeen, Patchen found employment in the steel mill where his father worked; later, he studied at the University of Wisconsin Experimental College. During the next few years, Patchen drifted across the United States, supporting himself with odd jobs, until 1936, when he received a Guggenheim Fellowship. Despite falling prey to a debilitating spinal illness (he was bedridden after 1960), Patchen wrote prolifically. In addition to over twenty volumes of his sometimes frenzied verse (by turns humorous or sinister), Patchen published two notable prose works, *The Journal of Albion Moonlight* (1941) and *Memoirs of a Shy Pornographer*. Moreover, he created over one-thousand "painted books"—one-of-a-kind hand-lettered booklets decorated with his own paintings. Patchen's *Collected Poems* was brought out by New Directions in 1968.

### Night Has Been as Beautiful as Virginia

This ends: entering the show of silence:
Voices gone: the outposts of glory given
Bare to stillness. Traps are sprung on day;
Corpse sprawls free, is spared a second's
Grace–blunted by dark the trees
Draw back, like ghostly badgers given
Homes whose profile needs a brighter earth,
      then, as we watch,
Like collapsible drinking-cups, they lunge
At space, in full gulp getting the first star.
Through hours, intent on fields within ourselves;
Exploring maps that lead from womb
To will of being here where every flower closed,
Where every use of light goes late to memory
And goal awaits tomorrow's massive towns

We hear the dark curve of eternity go coughing down the hills
No bird could stay this dangerous bough, no singing
Equal this
Our shield shall bear divorce of time and bring
O bring, as we watch in this dark
      like dawn
O bring proclaim the pity shock this hunger's timeless game.

### A Letter on the Use of Machine Guns at Weddings

Like the soldier, like the sailor, like the bib and tuck
    and bailer,
like the corner where we loiter, like the congressman
    and lawyer,
like the cop on the hill, like the lead in weary Will,
like the kittens in the water, like the names on Hearst's blotter,
like the guys and dames who laugh and chatter,
like the boys and girls who don't matter,
like the preacher and the Pope, like the punks who
    dish the dope,

like the hungry singing Home on the Range,
like Father Coughlin acting like Red Grange,
like the grumble of the tuba, like the sugar war in Cuba,
like the bill-collectors, like the Law-respecters,
like the pimps and prostitutes, like Mickey Mouse
            and Puss-in-Boots,
like the churches and the jails, like Astor's hounds and quails,
she's like you like her, now don't you try to spike her,
she's the nuts, she's a mile of Camel butts,
she's honey in the money, she's my pearl,
what am I offered for being alive and willing to marry the girl?
though her insides rumble and her joints are out of whack,
let's give her a whirl, why grumble or try to draw back?
though her hair is false and her teeth are yellow,
let's get chummy, let's all get a break. For what's a fellow
got at stake, for what's a guy to do
who hasn't the guts to deal with sluts, guys like me and you.


*Under the Green Ledge*

Under the green ledge
Sits a curious thing (I am walking
            through the snow. Two men
            with rifles follow at the distance
            of a long yell. Their eyes are sleepy
            and they don't seem to hate me.)
It has a tin cross
On its head. One ear
Is shaped like a dog's
And hangs down into the water. An old woman
Pours cocoa into a china mug and feeds
Her infant son. He gurgles like a tiny engine
Designed to amuse angels. But this happens
In another country where only people live.
For under the green ledge
Sits an awesome thing (I turn around
            and the men begin at once to build
            a great cart. They have no horse; fools,

I think–O a fine strong cart–but
what will pull and what will race
them round this ancient world! Then
I feel the shafts against my ribs
and I set off at a nervy clip–as
they sing and O they sing: "Blow away
the morning dew, the dew, and the dew,
blow away the morning dew; how sweet
the winds do blow!") Under the green ledge
Squats a curious thing (All the greenery and
All that's of the sea and of the land and of snow
That falls on my cold face; *and this heart*
Thus the taste of blood
The whip!
And I am running upon the world O
Sing blow away. The two men shine their rifles
On the velvet rag of my fear. Where running?
Whence the chase and the prized award?)
Men kill. Under the green ledge
I huddle with what life I can steal.


*An Examination into Life and Death*

Someone has fallen to the earth
Beneath the white tree.
As often as I say life I am confronted
By that falling O I am determined now
To grow within my saying until I see God
        until my branches grow again
        on the Tree O until my branches
        bloom again on that rootless Tree . . .
I am determined to turn my pattern
Into the costly rooms of the tempest:
To write my storm-name across the world.
Do you see him lying there? On his head
The surpassing climates lean; his mouth
Has the countenance of my saying O warm
And clothed in strength his body was

That is cold now. Written to the end that I may
Bury what is no longer of his element
            (was he of houses and sand towers
            of fruit on broken stems, dry dead flowers
            on a blood-sticky table O did he grow
            upon his rightful Tree, upon his Tree
            that alone covers him now) . . .
I make my peace with the mystery.
But where have the fallen gone?
O what hardens when all is so still and kind
In the manifold rooms of the dead? The first cry
Will be mine, God, O the first cry will be mine!
*I am the man all men would be.*
*I have opened.*
*These are my forms; this is my soil:*
*In the beginning there was light*
*And I held my hands to cover it out*
*But they came—my quest found bodies*
*In the hills whence the earth formed;*
*Bodies which no one has seen*
        *O some are flaming now*
        *they lift up the sun to new grounds*
*Where the eye of God walks serene and allknowing.*
O meaning is a fool's disguise!
Deprived of his clay position
Man fondles the shells of darkness
Where his real life waits.
I think that the fallen of earth
Are alive in the original world.
No one has really fallen
Whose house was prepared by fire.
Beneath the Life-Tree
The still figures rise to their sun,
And they are enveloped in skins of joy O they fall not
As we fall who are not yet arrived to taste journeys.
Do you see me lying here? On my heart
The uncaring heavens lean . . .
What can I believe!

*I am the voice all men hear.*
*I have been cleaned.*
*These are my people; this is my haven:*
*At the end there shall be light*
*And you will welcome the perfections*
*Of an endless world in which nothing is stained*
    *where you will dwell in wonder*
    *beneath the freed suns of your eight senses*
    *O where you will die not as they of living*
    *die who are not yet prepared to receive God.*
I make my place in the mystery.
I am the branch surely fallen from that rootless Tree.

.    .    .    .    .    .

When the one thing is completed,
The other may grow.
Each acts on his own nature,
And it is not necessary to die
If death be not present in you.
No one has really departed
Who was himself a beginning.
What collects in the human cave
Harbors the waters of birth.
Those who do understand this
Are wiser than any evil or good.
God is wiser than nature
Because it is unnatural to be God.

.    .    .    .    .    .

All sounds
All cryings
All events
All colors
Are His. He belongs nowhere.
He is the Being all men are kind to O He kills
For death is the eye which alone sees His Kingdom
For death is His eye.

## Saturday Night in the Parthenon

Tiny green birds skate over the surface of the room.
A naked girl prepares a basin with steaming water,
And in the corner away from the hearth, the red wheels
Of an up-ended chariot slowly turn.
After a long moment, the door to the other world opens
And the golden figure of a man appears. He stands
Ruddy as a salmon beside the niche where are kept
The keepsakes of the Prince of Earth; then sadly, drawing
A hammer out of his side, he advances to an oaken desk,
And being careful to strike in exact fury, pounds it to bits.
Another woman has by now taken her station
Beside the bubbling tub.
Her legs are covered with a silken blue fur,
Which in places above the knees
Grows to the thickness of a lion's mane.
The upper sphere of her chest
Is gathered into huge creases by two jeweled pins.
Transparent little boots reveal toes
Which an angel could want.
Beneath her on the floor a beautiful cinnamon cat
Plays with a bunch of yellow grapes, running
Its paws in and out like a boy being a silly king.
Her voice is round and white as she says:
"Your bath is ready, darling. Don't wait too long."
But he has already drawn away to the window
And through its circular opening looks,
As a man into the pages of his death.
"Terrible horsemen are setting fire to the earth.
Houses are burning . . . the people fly before
The red spears of a speckled madness . . ."
"Please, dear," interrupts the original woman,
"We cannot help them . . . Under the cancerous foot
Of their hatred, they were born to perish–
Like beasts in a well of spiders . . .
Come now, sweet; the water will get cold."
A little wagon pulled by foxes lowers from the ceiling.
Three men are seated on its cushions which breathe

Like purple breasts. The head of one is tipped
To the right, where, on a bed of snails, a radiant child
Is crowing sleepily; the heads of the other two are turned
Upward, as though in contemplation
Of an authority which is not easily apprehended.
Yet they act as one, lifting the baby from its rosy perch,
And depositing it gently in the tub.
The water hisses over its scream . . . a faint smell
Of horror floats up. Then the three withdraw
With their hapless burden, and the tinny bark
Of the foxes dies on the air.
"It hasn't grown cold yet," the golden figure says,
And he strokes the belly of the second woman,
Running his hands over her fur like someone asleep.
They lie together under the shadow of a giant crab
Which polishes its thousand vises beside the fire.
Farther back, nearly obscured by kettles and chairs,
A second landscape can be seen; then a third, fourth,
Fifth . . . until the whole, fluted like a rose,
And webbed in a miraculous workmanship,
Ascends unto the seven thrones
Where Tomorrow sits.
Slowly advancing down these shifting levels,
The white Queen of Heaven approaches.
Stars glitter in her hair. A tree grows
Out of her side, and gazing through the foliage
The eyes of the Beautiful gleam—"Hurry, darling,"
The first woman calls. "The water is getting cold."
But he does not hear.
The hilt of the knife is carved like a scepter
And like a scepter gently sways
Above his mutilated throat . . .
Smiling like a fashionable hat, the furry girl
Walks quickly to the tub, and throwing off
Her stained gown, eels into the water.
The other watches her sorrowfully; then,
Without haste, as one would strangle an owl,
She flicks the wheel of the chariot—around
Which the black world bends . . .

without thrones or gates, without faith,
warmth or light for any of its creatures;
where even the children go mad–and,
As though unwound on a scroll, the picture
Of Everyman's murder winks back at God.

Farther away now, nearly hidden by the human,
Another landscape can be seen . . .
And the wan, smiling Queen of Heaven appears
For a moment on the balconies of my chosen sleep.

# WILLIAM EVERSON ("BROTHER ANTONINUS")   [Born 1912]

William Everson was born in Sacramento, California, and grew up in nearby Selma. He became an agnostic in his teens, having been raised as a Christian Scientist. After dropping out of Fresno College, Everson married and worked for a time as a farmer and laborer. He was drafted when World War II broke out, but he refused military service and was confined during the next several years in various work camps for conscientious objectors. It was during his stay in the Waldport, Oregon camp, surrounded by writers and artists, that Everson published his first poems–mimeographed on the Untide Press. After the war his marriage broke up, and he moved to the Bay area of California, where he was associated with Kenneth Rexroth's group of poets and anarchists; he continued to operate the Untide Press out of his backyard. Everson remarried and was introduced to Catholicism by his new wife. In 1948 he published *The Residual Years: Poems 1934-1948*, a volume that established him as a poet of national stature. A year later, he and his second wife separated in order to serve the Catholic Church. Everson joined the Catholic Worker Movement, a group dedicated to helping the unfortunates on San Francisco's skid row. In 1950, as Brother Antoninus, he entered the Dominican Order of Preachers and spent the next six years in study and introspection. In 1969, he left the Order and resumed his literary career.

### Orion

Remote and beyond, lonely farms on the shoulders of hills
Sleep in the night. Seaward-running rivers,
Draining the continental flanks,
Pour in the dark, pour down the mountains,
Suck silt from the plains.
On inland ridges timber stirs in the cloud,

And far down the channels of the southern sky
Those arctic-loving tern are crossing the islands.
Mist gathers; the long shores whiten;
The midnight stars on the central sea
Lure the morning stars over Asia.

Light seeps at the window;
A faded chart of the used season hangs on the wall.
There are mats, worn, the thin bed,
The bare stand holding its chipped jug.
Glow from the alley colors the room: a dull stain.
The tension strung in the nerves of the city
Trembles the night.

Under the crust the massive and dormant stone of the earth
Swings at the core; bulk turns;
The weight turning on the tipped axis hangs to that line;
Atom-smashing pressures war at the center
Straining the charged and furious dark.

We, come at the dead of night
To the stale air of a drab room
High on the edge of the empty street,
Feel under the wind of our own compulsion
Those seekers before in the drained ages,
Daring the dark, daring discovery in the shut rooms,
Secretly meeting at river's edge under scant stars.
They sought and were lucky and achieved fulfillment;
They hung at last on the old fury,

And ground with their loins,
And lay sprawling and nude with their hearts bursting,
Their emptied flesh,
The spent mouths gasping against the dark.

They pound in our limbs at the clenched future.
They drive us above them, beating us up from that dead time,
Thrusting us up to this hanging room,
This toppling night, this act of their need
Forming again from the sunken ages.

Orion! Orion! the swords of the sky!
Forever above the eastern peaks they rise and go over,
Burning and breaking in the random years.
Under their light and the lean of a roof
They eyes drown inward, the blind eyes sinking,
The blind mouths, the great blind currents of the blood
        pulsing and rising.
Here in the room the streams of compulsion
Have formed in the rhythm of these gathering loins;
And feeling behind them the tides of all being—
Betelgeuse his bulk, and the yeared light, and the high
        silence—
They suck into union,
A part in the torrent of those shattering stars,
And time and space a waveless sea, and the dying suns.
Beyond all the sources of that breeding light
They strike and go out,
To the presence inscrutable and remote awake at the last,
Music that sings at a star's death,
Or the nature of night, that has border nor bulk,
And needs nothing.

Sleep, flesh. Dream deeply, you nerves.
The storms of the north are over Alaska.
This seed of the earth,
This seed of the hungering flesh,
Drives in the growth of the dark.

### The Illusion

The low wind talks on the boards of the house,
Gains and recedes, night deepens.
And feeling it round you,
The touch of this peace on your full spirit,
You know the illusion: men in the world stronger than you
Bleeding under the roofs, falling under the wheels,
Pitching down from the sky to lie in the fields under blunt
    stars.
Hear in the night the long wail
Calling the cars to some roadside shambles.
Remember him who lay on the mountain,
Holding his shattered foot, and the axe.
Think of the torn mouths begging release down the groove of
    the years.
Sit in your peace, drinking your ease in a quiet room,
Soft in your dreams–and the men falling.

The cities are shining.
The great ships west in the welter of seas hunt out the islands.
You feel the high, impregnable ranges of earth leaning in
    darkness.
You feel the texture of your living flesh
Wince on the bone.

You rest in your peace.
They pitch and go down with the blood on their lips,
With the blood on the broken curve of their throats,
With their eyes begging.

You rest in the ease and fortune of your dreams, and they
    break.
In the solitary towns, on the long roads high in the folded hills
The night blows over them rushing and loud, and they fall.

## The Impossible Choices

No, not ever, in no time,
In none of the brooding age of the breed,
Have the wings of salvation
Enfolded in triumph the living self.
There are those who cough up the rot of their lungs;
There are those strengthless divers of the sea,
Their bleeding ears in the pressure;
Those leaned to the lash;
Women split by the butting heads of their sons—
And all those webbed in their own desire,
Dragged through the bleaches of every sensation,
Who never attain, and who die forsaken.

Against the outer extreme or the inner compulsion
The flesh crumbles and breaks.
The bone is not strong.
The riotous nerves drink their own death in the roiling air;
Or the endless North grins against them its ready muzzle,
And reaps what it can.

One seeing his shadow
Thrown on the shape of that double doom
Looks to his method,
Sorting the chaos of all endeavor
For the narrow moment between the acts.
Fronting lust and revulsion
He painfully fashions the mode of survival;
Between the intolerable climaxes
The blossom flowers before his eyes.

He turns in the end to a mean, a measure,
The impossible choices hung at his hands,
And he leans between them,
Breathing an equinoctial air,
And lives in that weather at last.

## The Presence

Neither love, the subtlety of refinement;
Nor the outrider, thought;
Nor the flawed mirror of introspection,
Over all the age labored up from the ape,
Let light down that dark.
In the wilderness between skin and bone
There bulges the presence we do not know.
In the spun space between minute and minute
The will collapses;
The shape stoops in the mind, hairy and thick;
And the norms vanish,
The modes of arrest and the taut adjustments
Whirl down the years.

Women giving themselves in the summer nights to unknown
    men
Seek only the male hunger,
The masculine flesh;
Locking their knees round those dark loins
They couple in lust,
Are left in the weeds depleted and gasping,
Their bellies burdened with strange seed.

And those, cold and imperious, forging their lives,
Nursing their bitter precepts of will,
Enduring years of denial, years of restraint—
They too, they too will know in a bursting night
Their blood and nerve and their smothered need
Erupting like lava,
Their beasts' bodies doubled and lewd,
The gross voice of incontinence
Bawling along the vein.

They will lift up their knees
And that slogging plough will find the low furrow.
They will bear against it their gaped wombs,
Driving their flanks and their bending backs,

Driving their loins,
Throwing their bellowing flesh on the tool
That eases the rutting sow.

In the anguished awareness of all that it means
They will labor against it,
Seeking to kill in one ruinous act
The failed years, the spent endeavor.
Sobbing and lost they will plunge with their groins,
And fall broken down the dark.

They will be used;
And bleeding, will find it cold comfort to know
That what they went down to is greater than they had ever
      feared;
Than they dreamed;
Greater than their stubborn pride,
Or their pitiful will,
Or their racked bodies;
As great almost as that which watches beyond the bone,
And puts out the eyes,
And blackens in time the faces.


### The Residual Years

As long as we looked lay the low country.
As long as we looked
Were the ranchos miled in their open acres,
The populous oaks and the weedy weirs.
There were birds in the rushes.

And deep in the grass stood the silent cattle.
And all about us the leveled light.
Roads bent to the bogs;
Fenced from the fields they wound in the marshes.
We saw slim-legged horses.
We saw time in the air.

We saw indeed to the held heart of an older order,
That neither our past nor that of our fathers
Knew part in the forming:
An expansive mode remarked through the waste of residual
    years,
Large in its outline,
Turning up from its depth these traces and wisps
That hung yet on through a cultural close
We had thought too faint to recapture.


*Eastward the Armies*

Eastward the armies;
The rumorous dawns seep with the messages of invasion;
The hordes that were held so long in their hate
Are loosed in release.
The South shakes,
The armies awaken;
High in the domed and frozen North the armies engage;
They grope through the hills to the hooded passes;
They meet in the blue and bitter dawns,
And break up in the snow.
To the West: war, war,
The lines down,
The borders broken,
The cities each in its isolation,
Awaiting its end.

Now in my ear shakes the surly sound of the wedge-winged
    planes,
Their anger brooding and breaking across the fields,
Ignorant, snug in their bumbling idiot dream,
Unconscious of tact,
Unconscious of love and its merciful uses,
Unconscious even of time,
Warped in its error,
And sprawled in exhaustion behind them.

## Under a Keeping Spring

Under a keeping spring, that country,
Its hills green-headed, its swales water-delled–
A land, you would say, of great softnesses
Any month of the year;
But now, rains into June, drenchers,
The earth steeped in the mortal languor of wetness,
And the swaddling bands of sea-deriving fog
Huddling it in.

It is all out of season, all extra.
In the flush-full gulches the lank weeds flourish,
Quaking grass becks its rustling pod.
Everywhere on the upland meadow
Oat glistens, filaree and jacalac toss to the wind,
While the pale owl's-clover thrives in the pasture.
It is all extra. The cows browse on through the hour of
    milking:
They have to be driven.

And one thinks with a kind of wild exultance:
What a bringing down there is going to be when the sun gets
    to it!
What a scorching-over July will make!
For as the mind loves luxury,
But drives through its cloy to a strict extreme,
So now, impatient for summer,
It flares with the scything stroke of the sun
Toward a mown finale.

One week of that weather,
Give it ten good days;
And autumn will enter on all as it was:
Chewed over, eaten down, gnawn to a stubble;
And every seed, dry through the germ,
Knuckled up for a rain.

### End of Summer

The Berlin Airlift, 1948

Something that woke me out of sleep
Got me up in the pinch of night to haunt the house.
There was a drench of moonlight,
Rare enough on this fog-sealed coast to draw me out.
It was still September,
But looking up I saw fearful Orion,
His dog-star raging at his heel,
The fierce winter hunter
Rough on the innocent edge of summer;
And strangely beside them the great womanly planet,
Sad and maternal,
As if bearing some meaningful reassurance,
Waiting to speak.
It was like coming out of the depth of sleep on some deep
    divination.
Orion reared with his violent club,
Threatening the east,
And serenely beyond him the matronly planet.
What omen was meant?
What ominous warning and what grave reassurance?
Under the east the dawn lay waiting,
Breathing there on the edge of entry,
This much I knew.
And took the portent back to bed
Where the heavy hours could shape the oath
A million deaths might certify
Or a million lives reject.

## In the Dream's Recess

*Let from no earth-engendered thing your friendship be*
*    forsworn.*
Not from the Scorpion, that arcs its poison-shafted barb?
Not from the Spider nor the quick claw-handed Crab?
There is a place where all snake-natured things obtain,
Where squats the Toad: see there between his eyes
The carbuncular gleam break forth! The Sow Bug breeds
    there,
And the Sphinx Moth takes her vague compelling flight.

These are the dangerous kingdom's least inhabitants.
For deep in the groin of darkness, in the dream's recess,
Far back in the self's forbidden apertures,
Where clangs the door, comes forth the One.
Great prince, most baleful lord,
Clad in the adjuncts of his powerful craft;
The brimstone blazes on that unrelenting brow.

How may the soul, in horror hugged, make friends with him?
There lies a world of willfulness beyond one's best intent.
How may one reconcile it? There lies a universe of darkness
Far past the reaches of the wish. How may one
Civilize that obdurate realm? Deep down
The Scorpion lurks. The Salamander
Twists his chilly flesh. Deep down
The Horned Toad and the Crab consort.
All evil copulates. Each loathly thing
Peoples the dark with its sloth-gotten spawn.

Great God! Give me the cleansing power!
Scour me out with brightness! Make me clean!
The sullied presence crouches in my side,
And all is fearful where I dare not wake or dream.

## DELMORE SCHWARTZ   [1913-1966]

Delmore Schwartz was born in Brooklyn, New York, to a middle-class Jewish family. He studied philosophy at the University of Wisconsin and at Harvard, before receiving a degree from New York University in 1935. During the late thirties, Schwartz frequently published poetry in journals and magazines; his first volume of verse, *In Dreams Begin Responsibilities*, appeared in 1938 and won wide critical approval. In the next few years, he completed a play, *Shenandoah* (1941), and a book of criticism, *The Imitation of Life* (1942). Throughout his career, Schwartz supported his literary efforts by teaching writing at a number of colleges; he also served as editor of such journals as the *Partisan Review* and the *New Republic*. His *Summer Knowledge: Selected Poems 1938-1958* was awarded the Bollingen Poetry Prize in 1959, making him the youngest poet ever so honored. However, in the following years, Schwartz fell prey to mental illness. Though he wrote prolifically, he was tormented by doubts concerning the quality of his work and published few poems during the remaining years of his life.

### *In the Naked Bed, in Plato's Cave*

In the naked bed, in Plato's cave,
Reflected headlights slowly slid the wall,
Carpenters hammered under the shaded window,
Wind troubled the window curtains all night long,
A fleet of trucks strained uphill, grinding,
Their freights covered, as usual.
The ceiling lightened again, the slanting diagram
Slid slowly forth.
                    Hearing the milkman's chop,
His striving up the stair, the bottle's chink,
I rose from bed, lit a cigarette,
And walked to the window. The stony street
Displayed the stillness in which buildings stand,
The street-lamp's vigil and the horse's patience.
The winter sky's pure capital
Turned me back to bed with exhausted eyes.

Strangeness grew in the motionless air. The loose
Film grayed. Shaking wagons, hooves' waterfalls,
Sounded far off, increasing, louder and nearer.
A car coughed, starting. Morning, softly
Melting the air, lifted the half-covered chair
From underseas, kindled the looking-glass,
Distinguished the dresser and the white wall.
The bird called tentatively, whistled, called,
Bubbled and whistled, so! Perplexed, still wet
With sleep, affectionate, hungry and cold. So, so,
O son of man, the ignorant night, the travail
Of early morning, the mystery of beginning
Again and again,
                    while History is unforgiven.

## Father and Son

"From a certain point onward there is no longer any turn-
ing back. That is the point that must be reached."

                                        FRANZ KAFKA

*Father:*
On these occasions, the feelings surprise,
Spontaneous as rain, and they compel
Explicitness, embarrassed eyes—

*Son:*
Father, you're not Polonius, you're reticent,
But sure. I can already tell
The unction and falsetto of the sentiment
Which gratifies the facile mouth, but springs
From no felt, had, and wholly known things.

*Father:*
You must let me tell you what you fear
When you wake up from sleep, still drunk with sleep:
You are afraid of time and its slow drip,
Like melting ice, like smoke upon the air
In February's glittering sunny day.
Your guilt is nameless, because its name is time,
Because its name is death. But you can stop
Time as it dribbles from you, drop by drop.

*Son:*
But I thought time was full of promises,
Even as now, the emotion of going away—

*Father:*
That is the first of all its menaces,
The lure of a future different from today;
All of us always are turning away
To the cinema and Asia. All of us go

To one indeterminate nothing.

*Son:*
                                    Must it be so?
I question the sentiment you give to me,
As premature, not to be given, learned alone
When experience shrinks upon the chilling bone.
I would be sudden now and rash in joy,
As if I lived forever, the future my toy.
Time is a dancing fire at twenty-one,
Singing and shouting and drinking to the sun,
Powerful at the wheel of a motor-car,
Not thinking of death which is foreign and far.

*Father:*
If time flowed from your will and were a feast
I would be wrong to question your zest.
But each age betrays the same weak shape.
Each moment is dying. You will try to escape
From melting time and your dissipating soul
By hiding your head in warm and dark hole.
See the evasions which so many don,
To flee the guilt of time they become one,
That is, the one number among masses,
The one anonymous in the audience,
The one expressionless in the subway,
In the subway evening among so many faces,
The one who reads the daily newspaper,
Separate from actor and act, a member
Of public opinion, never involved.
Integrated in the revery of a fine cigar,
Fleeing to childhood at the symphony concert,
Buying sleep at the drugstore, grandeur
At the band concert, Hawaii
On the screen, and everywhere a specious splendor:
One, when he is sad, has something to eat,
An ice cream soda, a toasted sandwich,
Or has his teeth fixed, but can always retreat
From the actual pain, and dream of the rich.

This is what one does, what one becomes
Because one is afraid to be alone,
Each with his own death in the lonely room.
But there is a stay. You can stop
Time as it dribbles from you, drop by drop.

*Son:*
Now I am afraid. What is there to be known?

*Father:*
Guilt, guilt of time, nameless guilt.
Grasp firmly your fear, thus grasping your self,
Your actual will. Stand in mastery,
Keeping time in you, its terrifying mystery.
Face yourself, constantly go back
To what you were, your own history.
You are always in debt. Do not forget
The dream postponed which would not quickly get
Pleasure immediate as drink, but takes
The travail of building, patience with means.
See the wart on your face and on you friend's face,
On your friend's face and indeed on your own face.
The loveliest woman sweats, the animal stains
The ideal which is with us like the sky . . .

*Son:*
Because of that, some laugh, and others cry.

*Father:*
Do not look past and turn away your face.
You cannot depart and take another name,
Nor go to sleep with lies. Always the same,
Always the same self from the ashes of sleep
Returns with its memories, always, always,
The phoenix with eight hundred thousand memories!

*Son:*
What must I do that is most difficult?

*Father:*
You must meet your death face to face,
You must, like one in an old play,
Decide, once for all, your heart's place.
Love, power, and fame stand on an absolute
Under the formless night and the brilliant day,
The searching violin, the piercing flute.
Absolute! Venus and Caesar fade at that edge,
Hanging from the fiftieth-story ledge,
Or diminished in bed when the nurse presses
Her sickening unguents and her cold compresses.
When the news is certain, surpassing fear,
You touch the wound, the priceless, the most dear.
There in death's shadow, you comprehend
The irreducible wish, world without end.

*Son:*
I begin to understand the reason for evasion,
I cannot partake of your difficult vision.

*Father:*
Begin to understand the first decision.
Hamlet is the example; only dying
Did he take up his manhood, the dead's burden,
Done with evasion, done with sighing,
Done with revery.
     Decide that you are dying
Because time is in you, ineluctable
As shadow, named by no syllable.
Act in that shadow, as if death were now:
Your own self acts then, then you know.

*Son:*
My father has taught me to be serious.

*Father:*
Be guilty of yourself in the full looking-glass.

### The Sin of Hamlet

The horns in the harbor booming, vaguely,
Fog, forgotten, yesterday, conclusion,
Nostalgic, noising dim sorrow, calling
To sleep is it? I think so, and childhood,
Not the door opened and the stair descended,
The voice answered, the choice announced, the
Trigger touched in sharp declaration!

And when it comes, escape is small; the door
Creaks; the worms of fear spread veins; the furtive
Fugitive, looking backward, sees his
Ghost in the mirror, his shameful eyes, his mouth diseased.

### Parlez-Vous Français?

Caesar, the amplifier voice, announces
Crime and reparation. In the barber shop
Recumbent men attend, while absently
The barber doffs the naked face with cream.
Caesar proposes. Caesar promises
Pride, justice, and the sun
Brilliant and strong on everyone,
Speeding one hundred miles an hour across the land:
Caesar declares the will. The barber firmly
Planes the stubble with a steady hand,
While all in barber chairs reclining,
In wet white faces, fully understand
Good and evil, who is Gentile, weakness and command.

And now who enters quietly? Who is this one
Shy, pale, and quite abstracted? Who is he?
It is the writer merely, with a three-day beard,
His tiredness not evident. He wears no tie.
And now he hears his enemy and trembles,
Resolving, speaks: "Ecoutez! La plupart des hommes
Vivent des vies de désespoir silencieux,

Victimes des intentions innombrables. Et ça
Cet homme sait bien. Les mots de cette voix sont
Des songes et des mensonges. Il prend le choix,
Il prend la volonté, il porte la fin d'été,
La guerre. Ecoutez-moi! Il porte la mort."
He stands there speaking and they laugh to hear
Rage and excitement from the foreigner.

### Prothalamion

"little soul, little flirting,
   little perverse one
      where are you off to now?
little wan one, firm one
   little exposed one . . .
      and never make fun of me again."

Now I must betray myself.
The feast of bondage and unity is near,
And none engaged in that great piety
When each bows to the other, kneels, and takes
Hand and hand, glance and glance, care and care,
None may wear masks or enigmatic clothes,
For weakness blinds the wounded face enough.
In this sense, see my shocking nakedness.

I gave a girl an apple when five years old,
Saying, Will you be sorry when I am gone?
Ravenous for such courtesies, my name
Is fed like a raving fire, insatiate still.
But do not be afraid.
For I forget myself. I do indeed
Before each genuine beauty, and I will
Forget myself before your unknown heart.

I will forget the speech my mother made
In a restaurant, trapping my father there
At dinner with his whore. Her spoken rage

Struck down the child of seven years
With shame for all three, with pity for
The helpless harried waiter, with anger for
The diners gazing, avid, and contempt,
And great disgust for every human being.
I will remember this. My mother's rhetoric
Has charmed my various tongue, but now I know
Love's metric seeks a rhyme more pure and sure.

For thus it is that I betray myself,
Passing the terror of childhood at second hand
Through nervous, learned fingertips.
At thirteen when a little girl died,
I walked for three weeks neither alive nor dead,
And could not understand and still cannot
The adult blind to the nearness of the dead,
Or carefully ignorant of their own death.
—This sense could shadow all time's curving fruits,
But we will taste of them the whole night long,
Forgetting no twelfth night, no fete of June,
But in the daylight knowing our nothingness.

Let Freud and Marx be wedding guests indeed!
Let them mark out the masks that face us there,
For of all anguish, weakness, loss and failure,
No form is cruel as self-deception, none
Shows day-by-day a bad dream long lived
And unbroken like the lies
We tell each other because we are rich or poor.
Though from the general guilt not free
We can keep honor by being poor.

The waste, the evil, the abomination
Is interrupted. The perfect stars persist
Small in the guilty night,
                              and Mozart shows
The irreducible incorruptible good
Risen past birth and death, though he is dead.
Hope, like a face reflected on the windowpane,

Remote and dim, fosters a myth or dream,
And in that dream, I speak, I summon all
Who are our friends somehow and thus I say:

"Bid the jewellers come with monocles,
Exclaiming, Pure! Intrinsic! Final!
Summon the children eating ice cream
To speak the chill thrill of immediacy.
Call for the acrobats who tumble
The ecstasy of the somersault.
Bid the self-sufficient stars be piercing
In the sublime and inexhaustible blue.

"Bring a mathematician, there is much to count,
The unending continuum of my attention:
Infinity will hurry his multiplied voice!
Bring the poised impeccable diver,
Summon the skater, precise in figure,
He knows the peril of circumstance,
The risk of movement and the hard ground.
Summon the florist! And the tobacconist!
All who have known a plant-like beauty:
Summon the charming bird for ignorant song.

"You, Athena, with your tired beauty,
Will you give me away? For you must come
In a bathing suit with that white owl
Whom, as I walk, I will hold in my hand.
You too, Crusoe, to utter the emotion
Of finding Friday, no longer alone;
You too, Chaplin, muse of the curbstone,
Mummer of hope, you understand!"

But this is fantastic and pitiful,
And no one comes, none will, we are alone,
And what is possible is my own voice,
Speaking its wish, despite its lasting fear;
Speaking its hope, its promise and its fear
The voice drunk with itself and rapt in fear,

Exaggeration, braggadocio,
Rhetoric and hope, and always fear:

"For fifty-six or for a thousand years,
I will live with you and be your friend,
And what your body and what your spirit bears
I will like my own body cure and tend.
But you are heavy and my body's weight
Is great and heavy: when I carry you
I lift upon my back time like a fate
Near as my heart, dark when I marry you.

"The voice's promise is easy, and hope
Is drunk, and wanton, and unwilled;
In time's quicksilver, where our desires grope,
The dream is warped or monstrously fulfilled.
In this sense, listen, listen, and draw near:
Love is inexhaustible and full of fear."

This life is endless and my eyes are tired,
So that, again and again, I touch a chair,
Or go to the window, press my face
Against it, hoping with substantial touch,
Colorful sight, or turning things to gain once more
The look of actuality, the certainty
Of those who run down stairs and drive a car.
Then let us be each other's truth, let us
Affirm the other's self, and be
The other's audience, the other's state,
Each to the other his sonorous fame.

Now you will be afraid, when, waking up,
Before familiar morning, by my mute side
Wan and abandoned then, when, waking up,
You see the lion or lamb upon my face
Or see the daemon breathing heavily
His sense of ignorance, his wish to die,
For I am nothing because my circus self
Divides its love a million times.

I am the octopus in love with God,
For thus is my desire inconclusible,
Until my mind, deranged in swimming tubes,
Issues its own darkness, clutching seas
–O God of my perfect ignorance,
Bring the New Year to my only sister soon,
Take from me strength and power to bless her head,
Give her magnitude of secular trust,
Until she turns to me in her troubled sleep,
Seeing me in my wish, free from self-wrongs.

### Socrates' Ghost Must Haunt Me Now

Socrates' ghost must haunt me now,
Notorious death has let him go,
He comes to me with a clumsy bow,
Saying in his disused voice,
That I do not know I do not know,
The mechanical whims of appetite
Are all that I have of conscious choice,
The butterfly caged in electric light
Is my only day in the world's great night,
Love is not love, it is a child
Sucking his thumb and biting his lip,
But grasp it all, there may be more!
From the topless sky to the bottomless floor
With the heavy head and the fingertip:
All is not blind, obscene, and poor.
Socrates stands by me stockstill,
Teaching hope to my flickering will,
Pointing to the sky's inexorable blue
–Old Noumenon, come true, come true!

*Calmly We Walk Through This April's Day*

Calmly we walk through this April's day,
Metropolitan poetry here and there,
In the park sit pauper and *rentier*,
The screaming children, the motor-car
Fugitive about us, running away,
Between the worker and the millionaire
Number provides all distances,
It is Nineteen Thirty-Seven now,
Many great dears are taken away,
What will become of you and me
(This is the school in which we learn . . .)
Besides the photo and the memory?
(. . . that time is the fire in which we burn.)

(This is the school in which we learn . . .)
What is the self amid this blaze?
What am I now that I was then
Which I shall suffer and act again,
The theodicy I wrote in my high school days
Restored all life from infancy,
The children shouting are bright as they run
(This is the school in which they learn . . .)
Ravished entirely in their passing play!
(. . . that time is the fire in which they burn.)

Avid its rush, that reeling blaze!
Where is my father and Eleanor?
Not where are they now, dead seven years,
But what they were then?
                              No more? No more?
From Nineteen-Fourteen to the present day,
Bert Spira and Rhoda consume, consume
Not where they are now (where are they now?)
But what they were then, both beautiful;

Each minute bursts in the burning room,
The great globe reels in the solar fire,

Spinning the trivial and unique away.
(How all things flash! How all things flare!)
What am I now that I was then?
May memory restore again and again
The smallest color of the smallest day:
Time is the school in which we learn,
Time is the fire in which we burn.

### Dogs Are Shakespearean, Children Are Strangers

Dogs are Shakespearean, children are strangers.
Let Freud and Wordsworth discuss the child,
Angels and Platonists shall judge the dog,
The running dog, who paused, distending nostrils,
Then barked and wailed; the boy who pinched his sister,
The little girl who sang the song from *Twelfth Night*,
As if she understood the wind and rain,
The dog who moaned, hearing the violins in concert.
–O I am sad when I see dogs or children!
For they are strangers, they are Shakespearean.

Tell us, Freud, can it be that lovely children
Have merely ugly dreams of natural functions?
And you, too, Wordsworth, are children truly
Clouded with glory, learned in dark Nature?
The dog in humble inquiry along the ground,
The child who credits dreams and fears the dark,
Know more and less than you: they know full well
Nor dream nor childhood answer questions well:
You too are strangers, children are Shakespearean.

Regard the child, regard the animal,
Welcome strangers, but study daily things,
Knowing that heaven and hell surround us,
But this, this which we say before we're sorry,
This which we live behind our unseen faces,
Is neither dream, nor childhood, neither
Myth, nor landscape, final, nor finished,

For we are incomplete and know no future,
And we are howling or dancing out our souls
In beating syllables before the curtain:
We are Shakespearean, we are strangers.


## I Am to My Own Heart Merely a Serf

I am to my own heart merely a serf
And follow humbly as it glides with autos
And come attentive when it is too sick,
In the bad cold of sorrow much too weak,
To drink some coffee, light a cigarette
And think of summer beaches, blue and gay.
I climb the sides of buildings just to get
Merely a gob of gum, all that is left
Of its infatuation of last year.
Being the servant of incredible assumption,
Being to my own heart merely a serf.

I have been sick of its cruel rule, as sick
As one is sick of chewing gum all day;
Only inside of sleep did all my anger
Spend itself, restore me to my role,
Comfort me, bring me to the morning
Willing and smiling, ready to be of service,
To box its shadow, lead its brutish dogs,
Knowing its vanity the vanity of waves.

But when sleep too is crowded, when sleep too
Is full of chores impossible and heavy,
The looking for white doors whose numbers are
Different and equal, that is, infinite,
The carriage of my father on my back,
Last summer, 1910, and my own people,
The government of love's great polity,
The choice of taxes, the production
Of clocks, of lights, and horses, the location
Of monuments, of hotels and of rhyme,

Then, then, in final anger, I wake up!
Merely wake up once more,
                                        once more to resume
The unfed hope, the unfed animal,
Being the servant of incredible assumption,
Being to my own heart merely a serf.


### The Heavy Bear Who Goes with Me

"the withness of the body"

The heavy bear who goes with me,
A manifold honey to smear his face,
Clumsy and lumbering here and there,
The central ton of every place,
The hungry beating brutish one
In love with candy, anger, and sleep,
Crazy factotum, dishevelling all,
Climbs the building, kicks the football,
Boxes his brother in the hate-ridden city.

Breathing at my side, that heavy animal,
That heavy bear who sleeps with me,
Howls in his sleep for a world of sugar,
A sweetness intimate as the water's clasp,
Howls in his sleep because the tight-rope
Trembles and shows the darkness beneath.
–The strutting show-off is terrified,
Dressed in his dress-suit, bulging his pants,
Trembles to think that his quivering meat
Must finally wince to nothing at all.

That inescapable animal walks with me,
Has followed me since the black womb held,
Moves where I move, distorting my gesture,
A caricature, a swollen shadow,
A stupid clown of the spirit's motive,
Perplexes and affronts with his own darkness,

The secret life of belly and bone,
Opaque, too near, my private, yet unknown,
Stretches to embrace the very dear
With whom I would walk without him near,
Touches her grossly, although a word

Would bare my heart and make me clear,
Stumbles, flounders, and strives to be fed
Dragging me with him in his mouthing care,
Amid the hundred million of his kind,
The scrimmage of appetite everywhere.

### A Dog Named Ego, the Snowflakes as Kisses

A dog named Ego, the snowflakes as kisses
Fluttered, ran, came with me in December,
Snuffing the chill air, changing, and halting,
There where I walked toward seven o'clock,
Sniffed at some interests hidden and open,
Whirled, descending, and stood still, attentive
Seeking their peace, the stranger, unknown
With me, near me, kissed me, touched my wound,
My simple face, obsessed and pleasure bound.

"Not free, no liberty, rock that you carry,"
So spoke Ego in his cracked and harsh voice,
While snowflakes kissed me and satisfied minutes,
Falling from some place half believed and unknown,
"You will not be free, nor ever alone,"
So spoke Ego, "Mine is the kingdom,
Dynasty's bone: you will not be free,
Go, choose, run, you will not be alone."

"Come, come, come," sang the whirling snowflakes,
Evading the dog who barked at their smallness,
"Come!" sang the snowflakes, "Come here! and here!"
How soon at the sidewalk, melted, and done,
One kissed me, two kissed me! So many died!

While Ego barked at them, swallowed their touch,
Ran this way! And that way! While they slipped to the ground,
Leading him further and farther away,
While night collapsed amid the falling,
And left me no recourse, far from my home,
And left me no recourse, far from my home,

## During December's Death

The afternoon turned dark early;
The light suddenly faded;
The dusk was black although, elsewhere, the first star in the cold sky
   suddenly whistled,
And I thought I heard the fresh scraping of the flying steel of boys on
   roller skates
Rollicking over the asphalt in 1926,
And I thought I heard the dusk and silence raided
By a calm voice commanding consciousness:
*Wait: wait: wait as if you had always waited*
*And as if it has always been dark*
*And as if the world had been from the beginning*
*A lost and drunken ark in which the only light*
*Was the dread and white of the terrified animals' eyes.*
And then, turning on the light, I took a book
That I might gaze upon another's vision of the abyss of conscious-
   ness—
The hope, and the pain of hope, and the patience of hope and its
   torment, its astonishment, its endlessness.

## Once and for All

Once, when I was a boy,
Apollo summoned me
To be apprenticed to the endless summer of light and consciousness,
And thus to become and be what poets often have been,
A shepherd of being, a riding master of being, holding the sun-god's
   horses, leading his sheep, training his eagles,

Directing the constellations to their stations, and to each grace of
    place.
But the goat-god, piping and dancing, speaking an unknown tongue
    or the language of the magician,
Sang from the darkness or rose from the underground, whence arise
Love and love's drunkenness, love and birth, love and death, death
    and rebirth
Which are the beginning of the phoenix festivals, the tragic plays in
    celebration of Dionysus,
And in mourning for his drunken and fallen princes, the singers and
    sinners, fallen because they are, in the end,
Drunken with pride, blinded by joy.
And I followed Dionysus, forgetting Apollo. I followed him far too
    long until I was wrong and chanted:
"One cannot serve both gods. One must choose to win and lose."
But I was wrong and when I knew how I was wrong I knew
What, in a way, I had known all along:
This was the new world, here I belonged, here I was wrong because
Here every tragedy has a happy ending, and any error may be
A fabulous discovery of America, of the opulence hidden in the dark
    depths and glittering heights of reality.

## ROBERT HAYDEN   [1913-1980]

Robert Hayden was born in Detroit and graduated from the University of Michigan. From 1954 to 1955, he travelled throughout Mexico on a Ford Foundation Grant. His distinguished academic career included appointments as the Bingham Professor of English at the University of Louisville and poet-in-residence at the University of Washington. More recently, he was a member of the faculty at Fisk University. Although Hayden did not attract wide notice in America until the publication of his *Selected Poems* in 1966, he previously published a small volume in England. Hayden's poems deal with such subjects as the history of American slavery and the Bahai religion; his intense yet disciplined verse has brought him recognition as one of the finest Black poets of his generation.

*Electrical Storm*

God's angry with the world again,
the grey neglected ones would say;
He don't like ugly.
Have mercy, Lord, they prayed,
seeing the lightning's
Mene Mene Tekel,
hearing the preaching thunder's deep
Upharsin.
They hunched up, contracting in corners
away from windows and the dog;
huddled under Jehovah's oldtime wrath,
trusting, afraid.

I huddled too, when a boy,
mindful of things they'd told me
God was bound to make me answer for.
But later I was colleged (as they said)
and learned it was not celestial ire
(Beware the infidels, my son)
but pressure systems,
colliding massive energies
that make a storm.
Well for us. . . .

Last night we drove
through suddenly warring weather.
Wind and lightning havocked,
berserked in wires, trees.
Fallen lines we could not see at first
lay in the yard when we reached home.
The hedge was burning in the rain.
Who knows but what
we might have crossed another sill,
had not our neighbors' warning
kept us from our door?
Who knows if it was heavenly design
or chance

(or knows if there's a difference, after all)
that brought us and our neighbors through–
though others died–
the archetypal dangers of the night?

I know what those
cowering true believers would have said.

## Full Moon

No longer throne of a goddess to whom we pray,
no longer the bubble house of childhood's
tumbling Mother Goose man,

The emphatic moon ascends–
the brilliant challenger of rocket experts,
the white hope of communications men.

Some I love who are dead
were watchers of the moon and knew its lore;
planted seeds, trimmed their hair,

Pierced their ears for gold hoop earrings
as it waxed or waned.
It shines tonight upon their graves.

And burned in the garden of Gethsemane,
its light made holy by the dazzling tears
with which it mingled.

And spread its radiance on the exile's path
of Him who was The Glorious One,
its light made holy by His holiness.

Already a mooted goal and tomorrow perhaps
an arms base, a livid sector,
the full moon dominates the dark.

### Belsen, Day of Liberation

Her parents and her dolls destroyed,
        her childhood foreclosed,
she watched the foreign soldiers from
        the sunlit window whose black bars

Were crooked crosses inked upon
        her pallid face. "Liebchen,
Liebchen, you should be in bed."
        But she felt ill no longer.

And because that day was a holy day
        when even the dead, it seemed,
must rise, she was allowed to stay
        and see the golden strangers who

Where Father, Brother, and her dream
        of God. Afterwards
she said, "They were so beautiful,
        and they were not afraid."

### The Ballad of Sue Ellen Westerfield

She grew up in bedeviled southern wilderness,
but had not been a slave, she said,
because her father wept and set her mother free.
She hardened in perilous rivertowns
and after The Surrender,
went as maid upon the tarnished Floating Palaces.
Rivermen reviled her for the rankling cold
sardonic pride
that gave a knife-edge to her comeliness.

When she was old, her back still straight,
her hair still glossy black,
she'd talk sometimes
of dangers lived through on the rivers.

But never told of him,
whose name she'd vowed she would not speak again
till after Jordan.
Oh, he was nearer nearer now
than wearisome kith and kin.
His blue eyes followed her
as she moved about her tasks upon the Memphis Rose.
He smiled and joshed, his voice quickening her.
She cursed the circumstance. . . .

The crazing horrors of that summer night,
the swifting flames, he fought his way to her,
the savaging panic, and helped her swim to shore.
The steamer like besieged Atlanta blazing,
the cries, the smoke and bellowing flames,
the flamelit thrashing forms in hellmouth water,
and he swimming out to them,
leaving her dazed and lost.
A woman screaming under the raddled trees—
Sue Ellen felt it was herself who screamed.
The moaning of the hurt, the terrified—
she held off shuddering despair
and went to comfort whom she could.
Wagons torches bells
and whimpering dusk of morning
and blankness lostness nothingness for her
until his arms had lifted her
into wild and secret dark.

How long how long was it they wandered,
loving fearing loving,
fugitives whose dangerous only hidingplace
was love?
How long was it before she knew
she could not forfeit what she was,
even for him—could not, even for him,
forswear her pride?
They kissed and said farewell at last.

He wept as had her father once.
They kissed and said farewell.
Until her dying-bed,
she cursed the circumstance.


*Night, Death, Mississippi*

I.

A quavering cry. Screech-owl?
Or one of them?
The old man in his reek
and gauntness laughs—

One of them, I bet—
and turns out the kitchen lamp,
limping to the porch to listen
in the windowless night.

Be there with Boy and the rest
if I was well again.
Time was. Time was.
White robes like moonlight

In the sweetgum dark.
Unbucked that one then
and him squealing bloody Jesus
as we cut it off.

Time was. A cry?
A cry all right.
He hawks and spits,
fevered as by groinfire.

Have us a bottle,
Boy and me—
he's earned him a bottle—
when he gets home.

## II.

Then we beat them, he said,
beat them till our arms was tired
and the big old chains
messy and red.

*O Jesus burning on the lily cross*

Christ, it was better
than hunting bear
which don't know why
you want him dead.

*O night, rawhead and bloodybones night*

You kids fetch Paw
some water now so's he
can wash that blood
off him, she said.

*O night betrayed by darkness not its own*


*Day of the Dead*

(Tehauntepec)

The vultures hover wheel and hover
in skies intense as voyeur's gazing.

Cruciform black bells of clay
serenade Mr. and Mrs. Death
exposed in wedding clothes.

    Savage the light upon us,
    savage the light.

The graveblack vultures encircle afternoon,
transformed by steeps of flight
into dark pure images of flight.

Such pretty girls in Juchitán, señor,
and if one desires–

Death brings an almond sweetness
to the lips of children playing
with Jack-in-the-tomb and skulls of marzipan.

The tilting vultures glide
through causeway smoke to carrion.

In flowered shirt, androgynous,
the young man under palmleaf knives of sunlight
invites, awaits, obliquely smiles.

Such pretty girls, señor,
but if instead–

Barefoot Tehuanas in rhythmic jewels of gold
bear pails of marigolds upon their heads
to the returning dead.

Flee, amigo, for the dead are angry;
flee, lest the hands of dead men strike us down,
and the vultures pick our bones.

*Market*

Ragged boys
lift sweets, haggle
for acid-green
and bloody gelatins.
A broken smile
dandles its weedy
cigarette

over papayas too ripe
and pyramids
of rotting oranges.
Turkeys like feather–
duster flowers
lie trussed in bunchy smother.
The barefoot cripple
foraging crawls
among rinds, orts,
chewed butts, trampled
peony droppings–
his hunger litany
and suppliant before
altars of mamey,
pineapple, mango.
Turistas pass.
Por caridad, por caridad.
Lord, how they stride
on the hard good legs
money has made them.
Ay! you creatures
who have walked
on seas of money all
your foreign lives!
Por caridad.
Odor of a dripping
carcass moans
beneath the hot
fragance of carnations,
cool scent of lilies.
Starveling dogs
hover in the reek
of frying; ashy feet
(the twistfoot beggar laughs)
kick at them in vain.
Aloft, the Fire King's
flashing mask of tin
looks down with eyes
of sunstruck glass.

*Summertime and the Living . . .*

Nobody planted roses, he recalls,
but sunflowers gangled there sometimes,
tough-stalked and bold
and like the vivid children there unplanned.
There circus-poster horses curveted
in trees of heaven
above the quarrels and shattered glass,
and he was bareback rider of them all.

No roses there in summer—
oh, never roses except when people died—
and no vacations for his elders,
so harshened after each unrelenting day
that they were shouting-angry.
But summer was, they said, the poor folks' time
of year. And he remembers
how they would sit on broken steps amid

The fevered tossings of the dusk, the dark,
wafting hearsay with funeral-parlor fans
or making evening solemn by
their quietness. Feels their Mosaic eyes
upon him, though the florist roses
that only sorrow could afford
long since have bidden them Godspeed.

Oh, summer summer summertime—

Then grim street preachers shook
their tambourines and Bibles in the face
of tolerant wickedness;
then Elks parades and big splendiferous
Jack Johnson in his diamond limousine
set the ghetto burgeoning
with fantasies
of Ethiopia spreading her gorgeous wings.

## MURIEL RUKEYSER   [1913–1980]

Born in New York City, Muriel Rukeyser was the daughter of a building contractor. Her college education was accomplished at Vassar and Columbia University. In subsequent years, she lived in San Francisco, Chicago, New York, Indianapolis, and Portsmouth, New Hampshire. Her first book of poems appeared in 1935, entitled *Theory of Flight*. In this and the many volumes she published thereafter, Rukeyser demonstrated a flair for the dramatic in her powerful, emotionally-wrought verse. During her career, she was honored with a Guggenheim Fellowship, a grant from the National Academy, and the Harriet Monroe prize for verse. Besides poetry, Rukeyser produced prose, fiction, children's books, and biographies of the scientist Willard Gibbs and the little-known Elizabethan explorer Thomas Hariot. Her critical work, *The Life of Poetry,* explores the interrelationships between poetry and other disciplines. In addition, her translations of the Mexican poet Octavio Paz have been much praised.

*Poem Out of Childhood*

I

Breathe-in experience, breathe-out poetry :
Not Angles, angels : and the magnificent past
Not deep illuminations into high-school.
I opened the door into the concert-hall
and a rush of triumphant violins answered me
while the syphilitic woman turned her mouldered face
intruding upon Brahms. Suddenly, in an accident
the girl's brother was killed, but her father had just died :
she stood against the wall, leaning her cheek,
dumbly her arms fell, "What will become of me?" and
I went into the corridor for a drink of water.
These bandages of image wrap my head
when I put my hand up I hardly feel the wounds.
We sat on the steps of the unrented house
raining blood down on Loeb and Leopold,
creating again how they removed his glasses
and philosophically slit his throat.

 They who manipulated and misused our youth,
 smearing those centuries upon our hands,
 trapping us in a welter of dead names,
 snuffing and shaking heads at patent truth. . . .

We were ready to go the long descent with Virgil
the bough's gold shade advancing forever with us,
entering the populated cold of drawing-rooms;
Sappho, with her drowned hair trailing along Greek waters,
weed binding it, a fillet of kelp enclosing
the temples' ardent fruit :

      Not Sappho, Sacco.
Rebellion pioneered among our lives,
viewing from far-off many-branching deltas,
innumerable seas.

II

In adolescence I knew travellers
speakers digressing from the ink-pocked rooms,
bearing the unequivocal sunny word.

Prinzip's year bore us : see us turning at breast
quietly while the air throbs over Sarajevo
after the mechanic laugh of that bullet.
How could they know what sinister knowledge finds
its way among our brains' wet palpitance,
what words would nudge and giggle at our spine,
what murders dance?
These horrors have approached the growing child;
now that the factory is sealed-up brick
the kids throw stones, smashing the windows,
membranes of uselessness in desolation.

We grew older quickly, watching the father shave
and the splatter of lather hardening on the glass,
playing in sandboxes to escape paralysis,
being victimized by fataller sly things.
"Oh, and you," he said, scraping his jaw, "what will you be?"
"Maybe : something : like : Joan : of : Arc. . . ."
Allies Advance, we see,
Six Miles South to Soissons. And we beat the drums.
Watchsprings snap in the mind, uncoil, relax,
the leafy years all somber with foreign war.
How could we know what exposed guts resembled?

A wave, shocked to motion, babbles margins
from Asia to Far Rockaway spiralling
among clocks in its four-dimensional circles.
Disturbed by war we pedalled bicycles
breakneck down the decline, until the treads
conquered our speed and pulled our feet behind them,
and pulled our heads.
We never knew the war, standing so small
looking at eye-level toward the puttees, searching

the picture-books for sceptres, pennants for truth;
see Galahad unaided by puberty.

Ratat a drum upon the armistice,
Kodak As You Go : photo : they danced late,
and we were a generation of grim children
leaning over the bedroom sills, watching
the music and the shoulders and how the war was over,
laughing until the blow on the mouth broke night
wide out from cover.
The child's curls blow in a forgotten wind,
immortal ivy trembles on the wall:
the sun has crystallized these scenes, and tall
shadows remember time cannot rescind.

### III

Organize the full results of that rich past
open the windows : potent catalyst,
harsh theory of knowledge, running down the aisles
crying out in the classrooms, March ravening on the plain,
inexorable sun and wind and natural thought.
Dialectically our youth unfolds :
the pale child walking to the river, passional
in ignorance in loneliness demanding
its habitation for the leaping dream, kissing
quick air, the vibrations of transient light,
not knowing substance or reserve, walking
in valvular air, each person in the street
conceived surrounded by his life and pain,
fixed against time, subtly by these impaled :
death and that shapeless war. Listening at dead doors,
our youth assumes a thousand differing flesh
summoning fact from abandoned machines of trade,
knocking on the wall of the nailed-up power-plant,
telephoning hello, the deserted factory, ready
for the affirmative clap of truth
ricochetting from thought to thought among
the childhood, the gestures, the rigid travellers.

### Effort at Speech Between Two People

Speak to me.      Take my hand.      What are you now?
I will tell you all.      I will conceal thing.
When I was three, a little child read a story about a rabbit
who died, in the story, and I crawled under a chair :
a pink rabbit : it was my birthday, and a candle
burnt a sore spot on my finger, and I was told to be happy.

Oh, grow to know me.      I am not happy.      I will be open:
Now I am thinking of white sails against a sky like music,
like glad horns blowing, and birds tilting, and an arm about me.
There was one I loved, who wanted to live, sailing.

Speak to me.      Take my hand.      What are you now?
When I was nine, I was fruitily sentimental,
fluid : and my widowed aunt played Chopin,
and I bent my head on the painted woodwork, and wept.
I want now to be close to you.      I would
link the minutes of my days close, somehow, to your days.

I am not happy.      I will be open.
I have liked lamps in evening corners, and quiet poems.
There has been fear in my life.      Sometimes I speculate
On what a tragedy his life was, really.

Take my hand.      First my mind in your hand.      What are you now?
When I was fourteen, I had dreams of suicide,
and I stood at a steep window, at sunset, hoping toward death :
if the light had not melted clouds and plains to beauty,
if light had not transformed that day, I would have leapt.
I am happy.      I am lonely.      Speak to me.

I will be open.      I think he never loved me:
he loved the bright beaches, the little lips of foam
that ride small waves, he loved the veer of gulls:
he said with a gay mouth: I love you.      Grow to know me.

What are you now?      If we could touch one another,
if these our separate entities could come to grips,
clenched like a chinese puzzle . . . yesterday
I stood in a crowded street that was live with people,
and no one spoke a word, and the morning shone.
Everyone silent, moving. . . . Take my hand.      Speak to me.


## Theory of Flight

### Preamble

Earth, bind us close, and time ; nor, sky, deride
how violate we experiment again.
In many Januaries, many lips
have fastened on us while we deified
the waning flesh : now, fountain, spout for us,
mother, bear children : lover, yet once more :
in final effort toward your mastery.
Many Decembers suffered their eclipse
death, and forgetfulness, and the year bore round ;
now years, be summed in one access of power.
Fortresses, strengths, beauties, realities,
gather together, discover to us our wings
new special product of mortality.

Fortuitously have we gained loneliness,
fallen in waste places liberated,
relieved ourselves from weakness, loveliness :
remain unpitied now, never descend
to that soft howling of the prostrate mind.
Cut with your certain wings;      engrave space now
to you ambition : stake off sky's dimensions.
We have plunged on nightmares to destruction
too long; and learned aggression divides wind,
pale early Venus is signature of night
and wish gnawed clean by plans precurses flight.
Distinguish the metaphor most chromium clear
for distant calendars to identify :

Frail mouthings will fall diminished on old ears
in dusty whispers, light from extinctest stars
will let us sleep, nor may we replica
ourselves in hieroglyphs and broken things
but there is reproduction for this act
linking the flight's escape with strict contact.

. . . . .

Look! Be : leap ;
paint trees in flame
bushes burning
roar in the broad sky
know your color : be :
produce that the widenesses
be full and burst their wombs
riot in redness, delirious with light,
swim bluely through the mind
shout green as the day breaks
put up your face to the wind
FLY

chant as the tomtom hubbubs crash
elephants in the flesh's jungle
reek with vigor    sweat    pour your life
in a libation to itself
drink from the ripe ground
make children over the world
lust in a heat of tropic orange
stamp and writhe ; stamp on a wet floor
know earth    know water    know lovers
know mastery
FLY

. . . . .

Walks down the street
Kaleidoscope    a man
where patterns meet

his mind colored
with mirage
Leonardo's tomb
not in Italian earth
but in a fuselage
designed
in the historic mind
time's instrument
blue-print of birth.

.   .   .   .   .

We know sky overhead, earth to be stepped
black under the toes, rubble between our fingers,
horizons are familiar ; we have been taught colors
Rehearse these ; sky, earth, and their meeting-place,
confound them in a blur of distance, swallow
the blueness of guessed-at places, merge them now.
Sky being meeting of sky and no-sky
including our sources   the earth   water   air
fire to weld them : unity in knowing
all space in one unpunctuated flowing.
Flight, thus, is meeting of flight and no-flight.
We bear the seeds of our return forever,
the flowers of our leaving, fruit of flight,
perfect for present, fertile for its roots
in past   in future   in motility.

### The Speaking Tree

Great Alexander sailing was from his true course turned
By a young wind from a cloud in Asia moving
Like a most recognizable most silvery woman;
Tall Alexander to the island came.
The small breeze blew behind his turning head.
He walked the foam of ripples into this scene.

The trunk of the speaking tree looks like a tree-trunk
Until you look again.     Then people and animals
Are ripening on the branches;     the broad leaves
Are leaves;     pale horses, sharp fine foxes
Blossom;     the red rabbit falls
Ready and running.     The trunk coils, turns,
Snakes, fishes.     Now the ripe people fall and run,
Three of them in their shore-dance, flames that stand
Where reeds are creatures and the foam is flame.

Still Alexander stands.     He cannot turn.
But he is free to turn : this is the speaking tree,
It calls your name.     It tells us what we mean,

## KARL SHAPIRO   [Born 1913]

Karl Shapiro was born in Baltimore, Maryland. He attended the University of Virginia for a short time but left in order to devote his full attention to writing. The many long poems and plays written in the next few years were eventually destroyed by him, although a volume of short poems did appear in 1935. Subsequently, Shapiro returned to his studies at Johns Hopkins University. He had not yet completed his degree when he was inducted into the army, where he served in the South Pacific. During the war, Shapiro continued to write poetry, which his fiancée, Evelyn Katz, was able to get published; *V-Letter*, the book of poems that appeared in 1945, was awarded a Pulitzer Prize. Shapiro returned from the war with his literary reputation established. He served for a year as poetry consultant to the Library of Congress and went on to a distinguished teaching career at such institutions as the University of Nebraska, Johns Hopkins, and the University of California at Davis. During the fifties, he edited *Poetry* magazine and *Prairie Schooner*. Shapiro is known for his particularly moving accounts of the Jewish experience in America.

## Auto Wreck

Its quick soft silver bell beating, beating,
And down the dark one ruby flare
Pulsing out red light like an artery,
The ambulance at top speed floating down
Past beacons and illuminated clocks
Wings in a heavy curve, dips down,
And brakes speed, entering the crowd.
The doors leap open, emptying light;
Stretchers are laid out, the mangled lifted
And stowed into the little hospital.
Then the bell, breaking the hush, tolls once,
And the ambulance with its terrible cargo
Rocking, slightly rocking, moves away,
As the doors, an afterthought, are closed.

We are deranged, walking among the cops
Who sweep glass and are large and composed.
One is still making notes under the light.
One with a bucket douches ponds of blood
Into the street and gutter.
One hangs lanterns on the wrecks that cling,
Empty husks of locusts, to iron poles.

Our throats were tight as tourniquets,
Our feet were bound with splints, but now,
Like convalescents intimate and gauche,
We speak through sickly smiles and warn
With the stubborn saw of common sense,
The grim joke and the banal resolution.
The traffic moves around with care,
But we remain, touching a wound
That opens to our richest horror.
Already old, the question Who shall die?
Becomes unspoken Who is innocent?

For death in war is done by hands;
Suicide has cause and stillbirth, logic;
And cancer, simple as a flower, blooms.
But this invites the occult mind,
Cancels our physics with a sneer,
And spatters all we knew of denouement
Across the expedient and wicked stones.


### The Fly

O hideous little bat, the size of snot,
With polyhedral eye and shabby clothes,
To populate the stinking cat you walk
The promontory of the dead man's nose,
Climb with the fine leg of a Duncan-Phyfe
    The smoking mountains of my food
        And in a comic mood
    In mid-air take to bed a wife.

Riding and riding with your filth of hair
On gluey foot or wing, forever coy,
Hot from the compost and green sweet decay,
Sounding your buzzer like an urchin toy—
You dot all whiteness with diminutive stool,
    In the tight belly of the dead
        Burrow with hungry head
    And inlay maggots like a jewel.

At your approach the great horse stomps and paws
Bringing the hurricane of his heavy tail;
Shod in disease you dare to kiss my hand
Which sweeps against you like an angry flail;
Still you return, return, trusting your wing
    To draw you from the hunter's reach
        That learns to kill to teach
    Disorder to the tinier thing.

My peace is your disaster. For your death
Children like spiders cup their pretty hands
And wives resort to chemistry of war.
In fens of sticky paper and quicksands
You glue yourself to death. Where you are stuck
    You struggle hideously and beg,
        You amputate your leg
    Imbedded in the amber muck.

But I, a man, must swat you with my hate,
Slap you across the air and crush your flight,
Must mangle with my shoe and smear your blood,
Expose your little guts pasty and white,
Knock your head sidewise like a drunkard's hat,
    Pin your wings under like a crow's,
        Tear off your flimsy clothes
    And beat you as one beats a rat.

Then like Gargantua I stride among
The corpses strewn like raisins in the dust,
The broken bodies of the narrow dead
That catch the throat with fingers of disgust.
I sweep. One gyrates like a top and falls
    And stunned, stone blind, and deaf
        Buzzes its frightful F
    And dies between three cannibals.


*University*


To hurt the Negro and avoid the Jew
Is the curriculum. In mid-September
The entering boys, identified by hats,
Wander in a maze of mannered brick
    Where boxwood and magnolia brood
    And columns with imperious stance
    Like rows of ante-bellum girls
        Eye them, outlanders.

In whited cells, on lawns equipped for peace,
Under the arch, and lofty banister,
Equals shake hands, unequals blankly pass;
The exemplary weather whispers, "Quiet, quiet"
      And visitors on tiptoe leave
      For the raw North, the unfinished West,
      As the young, detecting an advantage,
          Practice a face.

Where, on their separate hill, the colleges,
Like manor houses of an older law,
Gaze down embankments on a land in fee,
The Deans, dry spinsters over family plate,
      Ring out the English name like coin,
      Humor the snob and lure the lout.
      Within the precincts of this world
          Poise is a club.

But on the neighboring range, misty and high,
The past is absolute: some luckless race
Dull with inbreeding and conformity
Wears out its heart, and comes barefoot and bad
      For charity or jail. The scholar
      Sanctions their obsolete disease;
      The gentleman revolts with shame
          At his ancestor.

And the true nobleman, once a democrat,
Sleeps on his private mountain. He was one
Whose thought was shapely and whose dream was broad;
This school he held his art and epitaph.
      But now it takes from him his name,
      Falls open like a dishonest look,
      And shows us, rotted and endowed,
          Its senile pleasure.

*Troop Train*

It stops the town we come through. Workers raise
Their oily arms in good salute and grin.
Kids scream as at a circus. Business men
Glance hopefully and go their measured way.
And women standing at their dumbstruck door
More slowly wave and seem to warn us back,
As if a tear blinding the course of war
Might once dissolve our iron in their sweet wish.

Fruit of the world, O clustered on ourselves
We hang as from a cornucopia
In total friendliness, with faces bunched
To spray the streets with catcalls and with leers.
A bottle smashes on the moving ties
And eyes fixed on a lady smiling pink
Stretch like a rubber-band and snap and sting
The mouth that wants the drink-of-water kiss.

And on through crummy continents and days,
Deliberate, grimy, slightly drunk we crawl,
The good-bad boys of circumstance and chance,
Whose bucket-helmets bang the empty wall
Where twist the murdered bodies of our packs
Next to the guns that only seem themselves.
And distance like a strap adjusted shrinks,
Tighten across the shoulder and holds firm.

Here is a deck of cards; out of this hand
Dealer, deal me my luck, a pair of bulls,
The right draw to a flush, the one-eyed jack.
Diamonds and hearts are red but spades are black,
And spades are spades and clubs are clovers–black.
But deal me winners, souvenirs of peace.
This stands to reason and arithmetic,
Luck also travels and not all come back.

Trains lead to ships and ships to death or trains,
And trains to death or trucks, and trucks to death,
Or trucks lead to the march, the march to death,
Or that survival which is all our hope;
And death leads back to trucks and trains and ships,
But life leads to the march, O flag! at last
The place of life found after trains and death–
Nightfall of nations brilliant after war.


## The Gun

You were angry and manly to shatter the sleep of your throat;
The kiss of your blast is upon me, O friend of my fear,
And I savour your breath like a perfume as salt and austere
As the scent of the thunder of heaven that brims in the moat!

I grip you. We lie on the ground in the thongs of our clasp
And we stare like the hunter who starts at a tenuous cry;
We have wounded the wind with a wire and stung in the sky
A white hole that is small and unseen as the bite of the asp.

The smooth of your cheek–Do you sight from the depth of your eye
More faultless than vision, more true than the aiming of stars?
Is the heart of your hatred the target of redness of Mars
Or the roundness of heart of the one who must stumble and die?

O the valley is silent and shocked. I absolve from your name
The exaction of murder, my gun. It is I who have killed.
It is I whose enjoyment of horror is fine and fulfilled.
You are only the toy of my terror, my emblem of blame.

Come with me. We shall creep for his eyes like the sweat of my skin,
For the wind is repaired and the fallen is calling for breath.
You are only the means of the practical humor of death
Which is savage to punish the dead for the sake of my sin!

### Lord, I Have Seen Too Much

Lord, I have seen too much for one who sat
In quiet at his window's luminous eye
And puzzled over house and street and sky,
Safe only in the narrowest habitat;
Who studied peace as if the world were flat,
The edge of nature linear and dry,
But faltered at each brilliant entity
Drawn like a prize from some magician's hat.

Too suddenly this lightning is disclosed:
Lord, in a day the vacuum of Hell,
The mouth of blood, the ocean's ragged jaw,
More than embittered Adam ever saw
When driven from Eden to the East to dwell,
The lust of godhead hideously exposed!

### Jew

The name is immortal but only the name, for the rest
Is a nose that can change in the weathers of time or persist
Or die out in confusion or model itself on the best.

But the name is a language itself that is whispered and hissed
Through the houses of ages, and ever a language the same,
And ever and ever a blow on our heart like a fist.

And this last of our dream in the desert, O curse of our name,
Is immortal as Abraham's voice in our fragment of prayer
Adonai, Adonai, for our bondage of murder and shame!

And the word for the murder of God will cry out on the air
Though the race is no more and the temples are closed of our will
And the peace is made fast on the earth and the earth is made fair;

Our name is impaled in the heart of the world on a hill
Where we suffer to die by the hands of ourselves, and to kill.

### The Synagogue

The synagogue dispirits the deep street,
Shadows the face of the pedestrian,
It is the adumbration of the Wall,
The stone survival that laments itself,
Our old entelechy of stubborn God,
Our calendar that marks a separate race.

The swift cathedral palpitates the blood,
The soul moves upward like a wing to meet
The pinnacles of saints. There flocks of thanks
In nooks of holy tracery arrive
And rested take their message in mid-air
Sphere after sphere into the papal heaven.

The altar of the Hebrews is a house,
No relic but a place, Sinai itself,
Not holy ground but factual holiness
Wherein the living god is resident.
Our scrolls are volumes of the thundered law
Sabbath by sabbath wound by hand to read.

He knows Al-Eloah to whom the Arab
Barefooted falls on sands, on table roofs,
In latticed alleys underneath the egg
On wide mosaics, when the crier shrills.
O profitable curse, most sacred rug,
Your book is blindness and your sword is rust.

And Judenhetze is the course of time;
We were rebellious, all but Abraham,
And skulked like Jonah, angry at the gourd.
Our days are captives in the minds of kings,
We stand in tens disjointed on the world
Grieving the ribbon of a coast we hated.

Some choose the ethics of belief beyond
Even particular election. Some

In bland memorial churches modify
The architecture of the state, and heaven
Disfranchised watches, caput mortuum,
The human substance eating, voting, smiling.

The Jew has no bedecked magnificat
But sits in stricken ashes after death,
Refusing grace; his grave is flowerless,
He gutters in the tallow of his name.
At Rome the multiplying tapers sing
Life endless in the history of art.

And Zion womanless refuses grace
To the first woman as to Magdalene,
But half-remembers Judith or Rahab,
The shrewd good heart of Esther honors still,
And weeps for almost sacred Ruth, but doubts
Either full harlotry or the faultless birth.

Our wine is wine, our bread is harvest bread
That feeds the body and is not the body.
Our blessing is to wine but not the blood
Nor to sangreal the sacred dish. We bless
The whiteness of the dish and bless the water
And are not anthropophagous to him.

The immanent son then came as one of us
And stood against the ark. We have no prophets,
Our scholars are afraid. There have been friars,
Great healers, poets. The stars were terrible.
At the Sadducee court he touched our panic;
We were betrayed to sacrifice this man.

We live by virtue of philosophy,
Past love, and have our devious reward.
For faith he gave us land and took the land,
Thinking us exiles of all humankind.
Our name is yet the identity of God
That storms the falling altar of the world.

### *V-Letter*

I love you first because your face is fair,
                  Because your eyes Jewish and blue,
Set sweetly with the touch of foreignness
Above the cheekbones, stare rather than dream.
Often your countenance recalls a boy
                  Blue-eyed and small, whose silent mischief
Tortured his parents and compelled my hate
                  To wish his ugly death.
Because of this reminder, my soul's trouble,
And for your face, so often beautiful,
                  I love you, wish you life.

I love you first because you wait, because
                  For your own sake, I cannot write
Beyond these words. I love you for these words
That sting and creep like insects and leave filth.
I love you for the poverty you cry
                  And I bend down with tears of steel
That melt your hand like wax, not for this war
                  The droplets shattering
Those candle-glowing fingers of my joy,
But for your name of agony, my love,
                  That cakes my mouth with salt.

And all your imperfections and perfections
                  And all your magnitude of grace
And all this love explained and unexplained
Is just a breath. I see you woman-size
And this looms larger and more goddess-like
                  Than silver goddesses on screens.
I see you in the ugliness of light,
                  Yet you are beautiful,
And in the dark of absence your full length
Is such as meets my body to the full
                  Though I am starved and huge.

You turn me from these days as from a scene
        Out of an open window far
Where lies the foreign city and the war.
You are my home and in your spacious love
I dream to march as under flaring flags
        Until the door is gently shut.
Give me the tearless lesson of your pride,
        Teach me to live and die
As one deserving anonymity,
The mere devotion of a house to keep
        A woman and a man.

Give me the free and poor inheritance
        Of our own kind, not furniture
Of education, nor the prophet's pose,
The general cause of words, the hero's stance,
The ambitions incommensurable with flesh,
        But the drab makings of a room
Where sometimes in the afternoon of thought
        The brief and blinding flash
May light the enormous chambers of your will
And show the gracious Parthenon that time
        Is ever measured by.

As groceries in a pantry gleam and smile
        Because they are important weights
Bought with the metal minutes of your pay,
So do these hours stand in solid rows,
The dowry for a use in common life.
        I love you first because your years
Lead to my matter-of-fact and simple death
        Or to our open marriage,
And I pray nothing for my safety back,
Not even luck, because our love is whole
        Whether I live or fail.

*Elegy for a Dead Soldier*

I

A white sheet on the tail-gate of a truck
Becomes an altar; two small candlesticks
Sputter at each side of the crucifix
Laid round with flowers brighter than the blood,
Red as the red of our apocalypse,
Hibiscus that a marching man will pluck
To stick into his rifle or his hat,
And great blue morning-glories pale as lips
That shall no longer taste or kiss or swear.
The wind begins a low magnificat,
The chaplain chats, the palmtrees swirl their hair,
The columns come together through the mud.

II

We too are ashes as we watch and hear
The psalm, the sorrow, and the simple praise
Of one whose promised thoughts of other days
Were such as ours, but now wholly destroyed,
The service record of his youth wiped out,
His dream dispersed by shot, must disappear.
What can we feel but wonder at a loss
That seems to point at nothing but the doubt
Which flirts our sense of luck into the ditch?
Reader of Paul who prays beside this fosse,
Shall we believe our eyes or legends rich
With glory and rebirth beyond the void?

III

For this comrade is dead, dead in the war,
A young man out of millions yet to live,
One cut away from all that war can give,
Freedom of self and peace to wander free.
Who mourns in all this sober multitude

Who did not feel the bite of it before
The bullet found its aim? This worthy flesh,
This boy laid in a coffin and reviewed–
Who has not wrapped himself in this same flag,
Heard the light fall of dirt, his wound still fresh,
Felt his eyes closed, and heard the distant brag
Of the last volley of humanity?

## IV

By chance I saw him die, stretch on the ground,
A tattooed arm lifted to take the blood
Of someone else sealed in a tin. I stood
During the last delirium that stays
The intelligence a tiny moment more,
And then the strangulation, the last sound.
The end was sudden, like a foolish play,
A stupid fool slamming a foolish door,
The absurd catastrophe, half-prearranged,
And all the decisive things still left to say.
So we disbanded, angrier and unchanged,
Sick with the utter silence of dispraise.

## V

We ask for no statistics of the killed,
For nothing political impinges on
This single casualty, or all those gone,
Missing or healing, sinking or dispersed,
Hundreds of thousands counted, millions lost.
More than an accident and less than willed
Is every fall, and this one like the rest.
However others calculate the cost,
To us the final aggregate is *one*,
One with a name, one transferred to the blest;
And though another stoops and takes the gun,
We cannot add the second to the first.

## VI

I would not speak for him who could not speak
Unless my fear were true: he was not wronged,
He knew to which decision he belonged
But let it choose itself. Ripe in instinct,
Neither the victim nor the volunteer,
He followed, and the leaders could not seek
Beyond the followers. Much of this he knew;
The journey was a detour that would steer
Into the Lincoln Highway of a land
Remorselessly improved, excited, new,
And that was what he wanted. He had planned
To earn and drive. He and the world had winked.

## VII

No history deceived him, for he knew
Little of times and armies not his own;
He never felt that peace was but a loan,
Had never questioned the idea of gain.
Beyond the headlines once or twice he saw
The gathering of a power by the few
But could not tell their names; he cast his vote,
Distrusting all the elected but not law.
He laughed at socialism; *on mourrait*
*Pour les industriels?* He shed his coat
And not for brotherhood, but for his pay.
To him the red flag marked the sewer main.

## VIII

Above all else he loathed the homily,
The slogan and the ad. He paid his bill,
But not for Congressmen at Bunker Hill.
Ideals were few and those there were not made
For conversation. He belonged to church

But never spoke of God. The Christmas tree,
The Easter egg, baptism, he observed,
Never denied the preacher on his perch,
And would not sign Resolved That or Whereas.
Softness he had and hours and nights reserved
For thinking, dressing, dancing to the jazz.
His laugh was real, his manners were homemade.

### IX

Of all men poverty pursued him least;
He was ashamed of all the down and out,
Spurned the panhandler like an uneasy doubt,
And saw the unemployed as a vague mass
Incapable of hunger or revolt.
He hated other races, south or east,
And shoved them to the margin of his mind.
He could recall the justice of the Colt,
Take interest in a gang-war like a game.
His ancestry was somewhere far behind
And left him only his peculiar name.
Doors opened, and he recognized no class.

### X

His children would have known a heritage,
Just or unjust, the richest in the world,
The quantum of all art and science curled
In the horn of plenty, bursting from the horn,
A people bathed in honey, Paris come,
Vienna transferred with the highest wage,
A World's Fair spread to Phoenix, Jacksonville,
Earth's capital, the new Byzantium,
Kingdom of man—who knows? Hollow or firm,
No man can ever prophesy until
Out of our death some undiscovered germ,
Whole toleration or pure peace is born.

## XI

The time to mourn is short that best becomes
The military dead. We lift and fold the flag,
Lay bare the coffin with its written tag,
And march away. Behind, four others wait
To lift the box, the heaviest of loads.
The anesthetic afternoon benumbs,
Sickens our senses, forces back our talk.
We know that others on tomorrow's roads
Will fall, ourselves perhaps, the man beside,
Over the world the threatened, all who walk:
And could we mark the grave of him who died
We would write this beneath his name and date:

### EPITAPH

Underneath this wooden cross there lies
A Christian killed in battle. You who read,
Remember that this stranger died in pain;
And passing here, if you can lift your eyes
Upon a peace kept by a human creed,
Know that one soldier has not died in vain.

### The Conscientious Objector

The gates clanged and they walked you into jail
More tense than felons but relieved to find
The hostile world shut out, the flags that dripped
From every mother's windowpane, obscene
The bloodlust sweating from the public heart,
The dog authority slavering at your throat.
A sense of quiet, of pulling down the blind
Possessed you. Punishment you felt was clean.

The decks, the catwalks, and the narrow light
Composed a ship. This was a mutinous crew

Troubling the captains for plain decencies,
A Mayflower brim with pilgrims headed out
To establish new theocracies to west,
A Noah's ark coasting the topmost seas
Ten miles above the sodomites and fish.
These inmates loved the only living doves.

Like all men hunted from the world you made
A good community, voyaging the storm
To no safe Plymouth or green Ararat;
Trouble or calm, the men with Bibles prayed,
The gaunt politicals construed our hate.
The opposite of all armies, you were best
Opposing uniformity and yourselves;
Prison and personality were your fate.

You suffered not so physically but knew
Maltreatment, hunger, ennui of the mind.
Well might the soldier kissing the hot beach
Erupting in his face damn all your kind.
Yet you who saved neither yourselves nor us
Are equally with those who shed the blood
The heroes of our cause. Your conscience is
What we come back to in the armistice.


## Lower the Standard

Lower the standard: that's my motto. Somebody is always putting the food out of reach. We're tired of falling off ladders. Who says a child can't paint? A pro is somebody who does it for money. Lower the standards. Let's all play poetry. Down with ideals, flags, convention buttons, morals, the scrambled eggs on the admiral's hat. I'm talking sense. Lower the standards. Sabotage the stylistic approach. Let weeds grow in the subdivision. Putty up the incisions in the library façade, those names that frighten grade-school teachers, those names whose U's are cut like V's. Burn the *Syntopicon* and *The Harvard Classics*. Lower the standard on classics, battleships, Russian ballet, national anthems (but

they're low enough). Break through to the bottom. Be natural as
an American abroad who knows no language, not even American.
Keelhaul the poets in the vestry chairs. Renovate the Abbey of
cold-storage dreamers. Get off the Culture Wagon. Learn how to
walk the way you want. Slump your shoulders, stick your belly
out, arms all over the table. How many generations will this take?
Don't think about it, just make a start. (You have made a start.)
Don't break anything you can step around, *but don't pick it up.*
The law of gravity is the law of art. You first, poetry second, the
good, the beautiful, the true come last. As the lad said: We must
love one another or die.


### *Randall Jarrell*

Randall, I like your poetry terribly, yet I'm afraid to say so. Not that my
    praise keeps you awake–though I'm afraid it does. I can't help
    liking them. I even like the whine, the make-believe whiplash
    with the actual wire in it. Once when you reviewed me badly (you
    must) I wrote you: "I felt as if I had been run over but not hurt."
    That made you laugh. I was happy. It wasn't much of a triumph
    but it worked. When people ask about you I am inclined to say:
    He's an assassin (a word I never use). I'm inclined to say: Why are
    you always yourself? Your love of Rilke–if it's love–your intima-
    cy with German and God knows what all, your tenderness and
    terrorization, your prose sentences–like Bernini graves, stagger-
    ingly expensive, Italianate, warm, sentences once-and-for-all.
    And the verses you leave half-finished in mid-air–I once knew a
    woman who never finished a sentence. Your mind is always at its
    best, your craft the finest craft "money can buy" you would say
    with a barb. I'm afraid of you. Who wouldn't be. But I rush to read
    you, whatever you print. That's news.


### *My Father's Funeral*

Lurching from gloomy limousines we slip
On the warm baby-blanket of Baltimore snow,
Wet flakes smacking our faces like distraught

Kisses on cheeks, and step upon the green
Carpet of artificial grass which crunches
Underfoot, as if it were eating, and come
To the canopy, a half-shelter which provides
A kind of room to enclose us all, and the hole,
And the camp chairs, and following after,
The scrolly walnut coffin
That has my father in it.

Minutes ago in the noncommittal chapel
I saw his face, not looking himself at all
In that compartment hinged to open and shut,
A vaudeville prop with a small waxen man,
"So cold," the widow said and shied away
In a wide arc of centrifugal motion,
To come again to stand like me beside,
In the flowerless room with electric candelabra.
If there is among our people any heaven,
We are rather ambiguous about it
And tend to ignore the subject.

The rabbi's eulogy is succinct,
Accurate and sincere, and the great prayer
That finishes the speech is simply praise
Of God, the god my father took in stride
When he made us learn Hebrew and shorthand,
Taught us to be superior, as befits
A nation of individual priests.
At my sister's house we neither pray nor cry
Nor sit, but stand and drink and joke,
So that one of the youngsters says
It's more like a cocktail party.

For Dylan's dandy villanelle,
For Sylvia's oath of damnation one reserves
A technical respect. To Miller's Willie
And Lewis's Babbitt I demur.
My father was writing a book on salesmanship
While he was dying; it was his book of poems,

Destined to be unpublished. He hadn't time
To master books but kept the house well stocked
With random volumes, like a ship's library,
Rows and rows of forgotten classics,
Books for the sake of having books.

My father in black knee-socks and high shoes
Holding a whip to whip a top upstreet;
My father the court stenographer,
My father in slouch hat in the Rockies,
My father kissing my mother,
My father kissing his secretary,
In the high-school yearbook captioned Yid,
In synagogue at six in the morning praying
Three hundred and sixty-five days for his mother's rest,
My father at my elbow on the bimah
And presiding over the Sabbath.

In the old forgotten purlieus of the city
A Jewish ghetto in its day, there lie
My father's father, mother and the rest,
Now only a ghetto lost to time,
Ungreen, unwhite, unterraced like the new
Cemetery to which my father goes.
Abaddon, the old place of destruction;
Sheol, a new-made garden of the dead
Under the snow. Shalom be to his life,
Shalom be to his death.

# WELDON KEES   [1914–1955]

Born in Beatrice, Nebraska, Weldon Kees was a fiction writer, critic, abstract expressionist painter, photographer, documentary film-maker, jazz pianist, composer, and poet. As a youth, he lived in New York, where he remained until 1951, when he moved to San Francisco. In painting, he was associated with both William de Koonig and Hans Hoffman. On July 18, 1955, he disappeared under mysterious circumstances. His car was found near the Golden Gate Bridge, and, while he had at times talked of suicide, he had also spoken of leaving the U.S. and living abroad under an assumed name. In 1960, *The Collected Poems of Weldon Kees* was published, edited by Donald Justice.

### For My Daughter

Looking into my daughter's eyes I read
Beneath the innocence of morning flesh
Concealed, hintings of death she does not heed.
Coldest of winds have blown this hair, and mesh
Of seaweed snarled these miniatures of hands;
The night's slow poison, tolerant and bland,
Has moved her blood. Parched years that I have seen
That may be hers appear: foul, lingering
Death in certain war, the slim legs green.
Or, fed on hate, she relishes the sting
Of others' agony; perhaps the cruel
Bride of a syphilitic or a fool.
These speculations sour in the sun.
I have no daughter. I desire none.

### Aspects of Robinson

Robinson at cards at the Algonquin; a thin
Blue light comes down once more outside the blinds.
Gray men in overcoats are ghosts blown past the door.
The taxis streak the avenues with yellow, orange, and red.
This is Grand Central, Mr. Robinson.

Robinson on a roof above the Heights; the boats
Mourn like the lost. Water is slate, far down.
Through sounds of ice cubes dropped in glass, as osteopath,
Dressed for the links, describes an old Intourist tour.
–Here's where old Gibbons jumped from, Robinson.

Robinson walking in the Park, admiring the elephant.
Robinson buying the *Tribune*, Robinson buying the *Times*.
  Robinson
Saying, "Hello. Yes, this is Robinson. Sunday
At five? I'd love to. Pretty well. And you?"
Robinson alone at Longchamps, staring at the wall.

Robinson afraid, drunk, sobbing Robinson
In bed with a Mrs. Morse. Robinson at home;
Decisions: Toynbee or luminol? Where the sun
Shines, Robinson in flowered trunks, eyes toward
The breakers. Where the night ends, Robinson in East Side
   bars.

Robinson in Glen plaid jacket, Scotch-grain shoes,
Black four-in-hand and oxford button-down,
The jeweled and silent watch that winds itself, the brief-
Case, covert topcoat, clothes for spring, all covering
His sad and usual heart, dry as a winter leaf.


### Robinson

The dog stops barking after Robinson has gone.
His act is over. The world is a gray world,
Not without violence, and he kicks under the grand piano,
The nightmare chase well under way.

The mirror from Mexico, stuck to the wall,
Reflects nothing at all. The glass is black.
Robinson alone provides the image Robinsonian.

Which is all of the room—walls, curtains,
Shelves, bed, the tinted photograph of Robinson's first wife,
Rugs, vases, panatellas in a humidor.
They would fill the room if Robinson came in.

The pages in the books are blank,
The books that Robinson has read. That is his favorite chair,
Or where the chair would be if Robinson were here.

All day the phone rings. It could be Robinson
Calling. It never rings when he is here.

Outside, white buildings yellow in the sun.
Outside, the birds circle continuously
Where trees are actual and take no holiday.

*January*

Morning: blue, cold, and still.
Eyes that have stared too long
Stare at the wedge of light
At the end of the frozen room
Where snow on a windowsill,
Packed and cold as a life,
Winters the sense of wrong
And emptiness and loss
That is my awakening.
A lifetime drains away
Down a path of frost;
My face in the looking-glass
Turns again from the light
Toward fragments of the past
That break with the end of sleep.
This wakening, this breath
No longer real, this deep
Darkness where we toss,
Cover a life at the last.
Sleep is too short a death.

*1926*

The porchlight coming on again,
Early November, the dead leaves
Raked in piles, the wicker swing
Creaking. Across the lots
A phonograph is playing *Ja-Da*.

An orange moon. I see the lives
Of neighbors, mapped and marred
Like all the wars ahead, and R.
Insane, B. with his throat cut,
Fifteen years from now, in Omaha.

I did not know them then.
My airedale scratches at the door.
And I am back from seeing Milton Sills
And Doris Kenyon. Twelve years old.
The porchlight coming on again.

# RANDALL JARRELL    [1914–1965]

Born in Nashville, Tennessee, Randall Jarrell spent a good part of his childhood in Long Beach, California, before returning to Nashville with his mother after his parents' divorce. He attended Vanderbilt University to do graduate work in English (having majored in psychology as an undergraduate). During World War II, he served for three years with the army air force in the Pacific and in Arizona. The books of verse he published in the aftermath of the war include *Little Friend* (1945) and *Losses* (1948); these contain some of the finest examples of war poetry to come out of the Second World War. Jarrell served for a time as poetry consultant for the Library of Congress and had a distinguished teaching career at such institutions as Kenyon College, the University of Texas, Sarah Lawrence College, and the Women's College of the University of North Carolina. Through his work as poetry editor of the *Nation*, and with critical works such as *Poetry and the Age* (1953), Jarrell established himself as one of the foremost critical minds of his time. Besides his poetry, Jarrell published the best-selling novel *Pictures from an Institution* (1954), a satire of academia. He also produced several children's books, including *The Bat-Poet*, along with translations of Grimm's fairy tales.

### The Knight, Death, and the Devil

Cowhorn-crowned, shockheaded, cornshuck-bearded,
Death is a scarecrow—his death's-head a teetotum
That tilts up toward man confidentially
But trimmed with adders; ringlet-maned, rope-bridled,
The mare he rides crops herbs beside a skull.
He holds up, warning, the crossed cones of time:
Here, narrowing into now, the Past and Future
Are quicksand.
          A hoofed pikeman trots behind.
His pike's claw-hammer mocks—in duplicate, inverted—
The pocked, ribbed, soaring crescent of his horn.
A scapegoat aged into a steer; boar-snouted;
His great limp ears stuck sidelong out in air;
A dewlap bunched at his breast; a ram's-horn wound
Beneath each ear; a spur licked up and out
From the hide of his forehead; bat-winged, but in bone;
His eye a ring inside a ring inside a ring
That leers up, joyless, vile, in meek obscenity—
This is the devil. Flesh to flesh, he bleats
The herd back to the pit of being.

In fluted mail; upon his lance the bush
Of that old fox; a sheep-dog bounding at his stirrup,
In its eyes the cast of faithfulness (our help,
Our foolish help); his dun war-horse pacing
Beneath in strength, in ceremonious magnificence;
His castle—some man's castle—set on every crag:
So, companioned so, the knight moves through this world.
The fiend moos in amity, Death mouths, reminding:
He listens in assurance, has no glance
To spare for them, but looks past steadily
At—at—
       a man's look completes itself.

The death of his own flesh, set up outside him;
The flesh of his own soul, set up outside him—
Death and the devil, what are these to him?

His being accuses him–and yet his face is firm
In resolution, in absolute persistence;
The folds of smiling do for steadiness;
The face is its own fate–*a man does what he must*–
And the body underneath it says: *I am.*


### The Venetian Blind

It is the first day of the world
Man wakes into: the bars of the blind
And their key-signature, a leaf,
Stream darkly to two warmths;
One trembles, becomes his face.
He floats from the sunlight
Into a shadowed place:
There is a chatter, a blur of wings–
But where is the edge of things?
Where does the world begin?
       His dreams
Have changed into this day, this dream;
He thinks, "But where am I?"
A voice calls patiently:
"Remember."
He thinks, "But where am I?"
His great limbs are curled
Through sunlight, about space.
What is that, *remember?*
He thinks that he is younger
Than anything has ever been.
He thinks that he is the world.

But his soul and his body
Call, as the bird calls, their one word–
And he remembers.

He is lost in himself forever.

And the Angel he makes from the sunlight
Says in mocking tenderness:
"Poor stateless one, wert thou the world?"
His soul and his body
Say, "What hast thou made of us, thy servants?
We are sick. We are dull. We are old."
"Who is this man? We know him not," says the world.

They have spoken as he would have made them speak;
And who else is there to speak?

The bars of the sunlight fall to his face.

And yet something calls, as it has called:
"But where am *I?* But where am *I?*"


*In the Ward:*
*the Sacred Wood*

The trees rise from the darkness of the world.
The little trees, the paper grove,
Stand woodenly, a sigh of earth,
Upon the table by this bed of life
Where I have lain so long: until at last
I find a Maker for them, and forget
Who cut them from their cardboard, brushed
A bird on each dark, fretted bough.
But the birds think and are still.
The thunder mutters to them from the hills
My knees make by the rainless Garden.
If the grove trembles with the fan
And makes, at last, its little flapping song
That wanders to me over the white flood
On which I float enchanted–shall I fall?
A bat jerks to me from the ragged limb
And hops across my shudder with its leaf
Of curling paper: have the waters gone?

Is the nurse damned who looked on my nakedness?
The sheets stretch like the wilderness
Up which my fingers wander, the sick tribes,
To a match's flare, a rain or bush of fire
Through which the devil trudges, coal by coal,
With all his goods; and I look absently
And am not tempted.
Death scratches feebly at his husk of life
In which I lie unchanging, Sin despairs
Of my dull works; and I am patient . . .
A third of all the angels, in the wars
Of God against the Angel, took no part
And were to God's will neither enemies
Nor followers, but lay in doubt:
                                        but lie in doubt.

There is no trade here for my life.
The lamb naps in the crêche, but will not die.
The halo strapped upon the head
Of the doctor who stares down my throat
And thinks, "Die, then; I shall not die"–
Is this the glitter of the cruze of oil
Upon the locks of that Anointed One
Who gazes, dully, from the leafless tree
Into the fixed eyes of Elohim?
I have made the Father call indifferently
To a body, to the Son of Man:
"It is finished." And beneath the coverlet
My limbs are swaddled in their sleep, and shade
Flows from the cave beyond the olives, falls
Into the garden where no messenger
Comes to gesture, "Go"–to whisper, "He is gone."

The trees rise to me from the world
That made me, I call to the grove
That stretches inch on inch without one God:
"I have unmade you, now; but I must die."

### The Death of the Ball Turret Gunner

From my mother's sleep I fell into the State,
And I hunched in its belly till my wet fur froze.
Six miles from earth, loosed from its dream of life,
I woke to black flak and the nightmare fighters.
When I died they washed me out of the turret with a hose.

### Losses

It was not dying: everybody died.
It was not dying: we had died before
In the routine crashes—and our fields
Called up the papers, wrote home to our folks,
And the rates rose, all because of us.
We died on the wrong page of the almanac,
Scattered on mountains fifty miles away;
Diving on haystacks, fighting with a friend,
We blazed up on the lines we never saw.
We died like aunts or pets or foreigners.
(When we left high school nothing else had died
For us to figure we had died like.)

In our new planes, with our new crews, we bombed
The ranges by the desert or the shore,
Fired at towed targets, waited for our scores—
And turned into replacements and woke up
One morning, over England, operational.
It wasn't different: but if we died
It was not an accident but a mistake
(But an easy one for anyone to make).
We read our mail and counted up our missions—
In bombers named for girls, we burned
The cities we had learned about in school—
Till our lives wore out; our bodies lay among
The people we had killed and never seen.
When we lasted long enough they gave us medals;
When we died they said, "Our casualties were low."

They said, "Here are the maps"; we burned the cities.
It was not dying–no, not ever dying;
But the night I died I dreamed that I was dead,
And the cities said to me: "Why are you dying?
We are satisfied, if you are; but why did I die?"


### Transient Barracks

Summer. Sunset. Someone is playing
The ocarina in the latrine:
You Are My Sunshine. A man shaving
Sees–past the day-room, past the night K.P.'s
Bent over a G.I. can of beets
In the yard of the mess–the red and green
Lights of a runway full of '24's.
The first night flight goes over with a roar
And disappears, a star, among mountains.

The day-room radio, switched on next door,
Says, "The thing about you is, you're *real*."
The man sees his own face, black against lather,
In the steamed, starred mirror: it is real.
And the others–the boy in underwear
Hunting for something in his barracks-bags
With a money-belt around his middle–
The voice from the doorway:"Where's the C.Q.?"
"Who wants to know?" "He's gone to the movies."
"Tell him Red wants him to sign his clearance"–
These are. Are what? Are.
                                    "Jesus Christ, what a field!"
A gunner without a pass keeps saying
To a gunner without a pass. The man
Puts down his razor, leans to the window,
And looks out into the pattern of the field,
Of light and of darkness. His throat tightens,
His lips stretch into a blinded smile.
He thinks, *The times I've dreamed that I was back* . . .
The hairs on the back of his neck stand up straight.

He only yawns, and finishes shaving.
When the gunner asks him, "When you leaving?"
He says: "I just got in. This is my field."
And thinks: *I'm back for good. The States, the States!*
He puts out his hand to touch it–
And the thing about it is, it's *real*.


*Siegfried*

In the turret's great glass dome, the apparition, death,
Framed in the glass of the gunsight, a fighter's blinking wing,
Flares softly, a vacant fire. If the flak's inked blurs–
Distributed, statistical–the bombs' lost patterning
Are death, they are death under glass, a chance
For someone yesterday, someone tomorrow; and the fire
That streams from the fighter which is there, not there,
Does not warm you, has not burned them, though they die.
Under the leather and fur and wire, in the gunner's skull,
It is a dream: and he, the watcher, guiltily
Watches the him, the actor, who is innocent.
*It happens as it does because it does.*
It is unnecessary to understand; if you are still
In this year of our warfare, indispensable
In general, and in particular dispensable
As a cartridge, a life–it is only to enter
So many knots in a window, so many feet;
To switch on for an instant the steel that understands.
Do as they said; as they said, there is always a reason–
Though neither for you nor for the fatal
Knower of wind, speed, pressure: the unvalued facts.
(In Nature there is neither right nor left nor wrong.)

So the bombs fell: through clouds to the island,
The dragon of maps; and the island's fighters
Rose from its ruins, through blind smoke, to the flights–
And fluttered smashed from the machinery of death.
Yet inside the infallible invulnerable
Machines, the skin of steel, glass, cartridges,

Duties, responsibilities, and–surely–deaths,
There was only you; the ignorant life
That grew its weariness and loneliness and wishes
Into your whole wish: "Let it be the way it was.
Let me not matter, let nothing I do matter
To anybody, anybody. Let me be what I was."

And you are home, for good now, almost as you wished;
If you matter, it is a little, almost, as you wished.
If it has changed, still, you have had your wish
And are lucky, as you figured luck–are, truly, lucky.
If it is different, if you are different,
It is not from the lives or the cities;
The world's war, just or unjust–the world's peace, war or
    peace;
But from a separate war: the shell with your name
In the bursting turret, the crystals of your blood
On the splints' wrapped steel, the hours wearing
The quiet body back to its base, its missions done;
And the slow flesh failing, the terrible flesh
Sloughed off at last–and waking, your leg gone,
To the dream, the old, old dream: *it happens,*
*It happens as it does, it does, it does–*

But not because of you, write the knives of the surgeon,
The gauze of the theatre, the bearded and aging face
In the magic glass; if you wake and understand,
There is always the nurse, the leg, the drug–
If you understand, there is sleep, there is sleep . . .
Reading of victories and sales and nations
Under the changed maps, in the sunlit papers;
Stumbling to the toilet on one clever leg
Of leather, wire, and willow; staring
Past the lawn and the trees to nothing, to the eyes
You looked away from as they looked away: the world out-
    side
You are released to, rehabilitated
*–What will you do now? I don't know–*
It is these. If, standing irresolute

By the whitewashed courthouse, in the leafy street,
You look at the people who look back at you, at home,
And it is different, different–you have understood
Your world at last: you have tasted your own blood.


### Pilots, Man Your Planes

Dawn; and the jew's-harp's sawing seesaw song
Plucks at the starlight where the planes are folded
At the lee of their blank, wind-whipped, hunting road–
A road in air, the road to nowhere
Turreted and bucketed with guns, long undermined
With the thousand necessary deaths that breathe
Like fire beside a thousand men, who sleep
Hunched in the punk of Death: slow, dreaming sparks
Who burrow through the block-long, light-split gloom
Of their great hangar underground and oversea
Into the great tanks, dark forever; past the steam
Of turbines, laundries–under rockets,
Bakeries, war-heads, the steel watch-like fish,
To the hull's last plates and atmosphere:
The sea sways with the dazed, blind, groping sway
Of the raw soul drugged with sleep, the chancy life
Troubling with dreams its wars, its own earned sea
That stretches year on year, death after death,
And hemisphere on blind black hemisphere
Into the stubborn corners of its earth.

Here in the poor, bleak, guessing haze of dawn
The giant's jew's-harp screeches its two notes
Over and over, over and over; from the roar
Of the fighters waved into the blazing clouds
The lookout lifts his scrubbed tetanic stare
Into the East of light, the empty day.
But on the tubes the raiders oscillate
A mile in every nine or thirteen seconds
To the target's first premonitory bursts;
To the boy with a ball of coffee in his stomach,

Snapping the great light buckles on his groin,
Shifting his raft's hot-water-bottle weight
As he breasts the currents of the bellowing deck
And, locked at last into the bubble, Hope,
Is borne along the foaming windy road
To the air where he alone is still
Above the world's cold, absent, searching roll.
The carrier meshed in its white whirling wake,
The gray ship sparkling from the blue-black sea,
The little carrier—erupts in flak,
One hammering, hysterical, tremendous fire.
Flickering through flashes, the stained rolling clouds,
The air jarred like water tilted in a bowl,
The red wriggling tracers—colonies
Whose instant life annexes the whole sky—
Hunt out the one end they have being for,
Are metamorphosed into one pure smear
Of flame, and die
In the maniacal convulsive spin
Of the raider with a wing snapped off, the plane
Trailing its flaming kite's-tail to the wave.
A miss's near, near bloom, a hill of foam,
Is bulged skyward, crashes back; crest after crest
Patterns the ships' cat's-cradle wakes, the racing
Swells that hiss outward from a plane's quenched flame:
There is traced in the thousand meetings of the grave
Of matter and of matter, man and man,
The print of the running feet upon the waves. . . .
The Jill threads her long, blind, unbearable
Way into fire (the waves lick past her, her whole sky
Is tracer and the dirt of flak, the fire
Flung from the muzzles riddling sea and sky),
Comes on, comes on, comes on; and the fighter flames to her
Through his own flak, the hammering guns
Stitch one long line along his wing, his gear
Falls, his dive staggers as his tracer strikes,
And he breaks off and somersaults into the sea.
Under the canopy's dark strangling green,
The darkening canopy, he struggles free

To float into the choking white, to breathe—
His huge leg floating and immovable,
His goggles blackened with his own bright blood—
On the yellow raft, to see his carrier
Still firing, but itself a fire, its planes
Flung up like matches from the stern's white burst.
Now rockets arch above the deck's great blaze,
Shells break from it, trail after trail; its steel
Melts in steam into the sea, its tanks explode
In one last overwhelming sound; and silently
The ship, a flame, sinks home into the sea.
The pilot holds his striped head patiently
Up out of the dancing smother of the sea
And weeps with hatred, longing, agony—
The sea rises and settles; and the ship is gone.
The planes fly off looking for a carrier,
Destroyers curve in their long hunting arcs
Through the dead of the carrier: the dazed, vomiting,
Oil-blackened and fire-blistered, saved or dying men
Cling with cramped shaking fingers to the lines
Lowered from their old life: the pilot,
Drugged in a blanket, straining up to gulp
From the mug that scrapes like chalk against his mouth,
Knows, knows at last; he yawns the chattering yawn
Of effort and anguish, of hurt hating helplessness—
Yawns sobbingly, his head falls back, he sleeps.


### Burning the Letters

(The wife of a pilot killed in the Pacific is speaking several years
    after his death. She was once a Christian, a Protestant.)

Here in my head, the home that is left for you,
You have not changed; the flames rise from the sea
And the sea changes: the carrier, torn in two,
Sinks to its planes—the corpses of the carrier
Are strewn like ashes on the star-reflecting sea;
Are gathered, sewn with weights, are sunk.

The gatherers disperse.
                              Here to my hands
From the sea's dark, incalculable calm,
The unchanging circle of the universe,
The letters float: the set yellowing face
Looks home to me, a child's at last,
From the cut-out paper; and the licked
Lips part in their last questioning smile.
The poor labored answers, still unanswering;
The faded questions–questioning so much,
I thought then–questioning so little;
Grew younger, younger, as my eyes grew old,
As that dreamed-out and wept-for wife,
Your last unchanging country, changed
Out of your own rejecting life–a part
Of accusation and of loss, a child's eternally–
Into my troubled separate being.

A child has her own faith, a child's.
In its savage figures–worn down, now, to death–
Men's one life issues, neither out of earth
Nor from the sea, the last dissolving sea,
But out of death: by man came death
And his Life wells from death, the death of Man.
The hunting flesh, the broken blood
Glimmer within the tombs of earth, the food
Of the lives that burrow under the hunting wings
Of the light, of the darkness: dancing, dancing,
The flames grasp flesh with their last searching grace–
Grasp as the lives have grasped: the hunted
Pull down the hunter for his unused life
Parted into the blood, the dark, veined bread
Later than all law. The child shudders, aging:
The peering savior, stooping to her clutch,
His talons cramped with his own bartered flesh,
Pales, flickers, and flares out. In the darkness–darker
With the haunting after-images of light–
The dying God, the eaten Life
Are the nightmare I awaken from to night.

(The flames dance over life. the mourning slaves
In their dark secrecy, come burying
The slave bound in another's flesh, the slave
Freed once, forever, by another's flesh:
The Light flames, flushing the passive face
With its eternal life.)
                              The lives are fed
Into the darkness of their victory;
The ships sink, forgotten; and the sea
Blazes to darkness: the unsearchable
Death of the lives lies dark upon the life
That, bought by death, the loved and tortured lives,
Stares westward, passive, to the blackening sea.
In the tables of the dead, in the unopened almanac,
The head, charred, featureless–the unknown mean–
Is thrust from the waters like a flame, is torn
From its last being with the bestial cry
Of its pure agony. O death of all my life,
Because of you, because of you, I have not died,
By your death I have lived.
                              The sea is empty.
As I am empty, stirring the charred and answered
Questions about your home, your wife, your cat
That stayed at home with me–that died at home
Gray with the years that gleam above you there
In the great green grave where you are young
And unaccepting still. Bound in your death,
I choose between myself and you, between your life
And my own life: it is finished.
                              Here in my head
There is room for your black body in its shroud,
The dog-tags welded to your breastbone, and the flame
That winds above your death and my own life
And the world of my life. The letters and the face
That stir still, sometimes, with your fiery breath–
Take them, O grave! Great grave of all my years,
The unliving universe in which all life is lost,
Make yours the memory of that accepting
And accepted life whose fragments I cast here.

# JOHN BERRYMAN    [1914–1972]

John Berryman was born near McAlester, Oklahoma, but his family moved to Tampa, Florida, when he was ten. Two years later his father shot himself to death. Berryman and his mother then lived for a time in Gloucester, Massachusetts, and later in New York City. His mother remarried (it is from his stepfather that he took his surname), but the union ended in divorce. Still, his stepfather paid for Berryman to attend a private school in Connecticut, after which he studied at Columbia University and Clare College of Cambridge University. He taught briefly at Wayne State, Harvard, and Princeton before settling at the University of Minnesota in 1955, where he remained until his death.

Berryman's first major collection of verse, *The Dispossessed*, appeared in 1948 and stands as one of the signal volumes of contemporary American verse. In the following years his reputation was to grow considerably, primarily owing to the success of his two long poems, *Homage to Mistress Bradstreet* (1956) and *The Dream Songs* (first published in 1964 as *77 Dream Songs*, and later, expanded to a total of 385 in the volume *His Toy, His Rest* [1968]). Indeed, at a time during which most poets were concentrating on rather brief utterances, Berryman flourished by allowing himself a wider canvas. In *Homage*, he addresses the resemblances between himself and the Puritan poetess; *The Dream Songs* sequence, loosely based on Walt Whitman's classic *Song of Myself*, offers the psychic biography of "Huffy Henry," a character similar in many ways to its creator. *The Dream Songs* made a celebrity of Berryman, bringing him first a Pulitzer Prize and later a National Book Award.

## The Moon and the Night and the Men

On the night of the Belgian surrender the moon rose
Late, a delayed moon, and a violent moon
For the English or the American beholder;
The French beholder. It was a cold night,
People put on their wraps, the troops were cold
No doubt, despite the calendar, no doubt
Numbers of refugees coughed, and the sight
Or sound of some killed others. A cold night.

On Outer Drive there was an accident:
A stupid well-intentioned man turned sharp
Right and abruptly he became an angel
Fingering an unfamiliar harp,
Or screamed in hell, or was nothing at all.
Do not imagine this is unimportant.
He was a part of the night, part of the land,
Part of the bitter and exhausted ground
Out of which memory grows.

                    Michael and I
Stared at each other over chess, and spoke
As little as possible, and drank and played.
The chessmen caught in the European eye,
Neither of us I think had a free look
Although the game was fair. The move one made
It was difficult at last to keep one's mind on.
'Hurt and unhappy' said the man in London.
We said to each other, The time is coming near
When none shall have books or music, none his dear,
And only a fool will speak aloud his mind.
History is approaching a speechless end,
As Henry Adams said. Adams was right.

All this occurred on the night when Leopold
Fulfilled the treachery four years before
Begun—or was he well-intentioned, more
Roadmaker to hell than king? At any rate,

The moon came up late and the night was cold,
Many men died–although we know the fate
Of none, nor of anyone, and the war
Goes on, and the moon in the breast of man is cold.


## The Dispossessed

'and something that . . that is theirs–no longer ours'
stammered to me the Italian page. A wood
seeded & towered suddenly. I understood.–

The Leading Man's especially, and the Juvenile Lead's,
and the Leading Lady's thigh that switches & warms,
and their grimaces, and their flying arms:

*our* arms, our story. Every seat was sold.
A crone met in a clearing sprouts a beard
and has a tirade. Not a word we heard.

Movement of stone within a woman's heart,
abrupt & dominant. They gesture how
fings really are. Rarely a child sings now.

My harpsichord weird as a koto drums
*adagio* for twilight, for the storm-worn dove
no more de-iced, and the spidery business of love.

The Juvenile Lead's the Leader's arm, one arm
running the whole bole, branches, roots, (O watch)
and the faceless fellow waving from her crotch,

Stalin-unanimous! who procured a vote
and care not use it, who have kept an eye
and care not use it, percussive vote, clear eye.

That which a captain and a weaponeer
one day and one more day did, we did, *ach*
we did not, *They* did . . cam slid, the great lock

lodged, and no soul of us all was near was near,–
an evil sky (where the umbrella bloomed)
twirled its mustaches, hissed, the ingenue fumed,

poor virgin, and no hero rides. The race
is done. Drifts through, between the cold black trunks,
the peachblow glory of the perishing sun

in empty houses where old things take place.

### The Poet's Final Instructions

Dog-tired, suisired, will now my body down
near Cedar Avenue in Minneap,
when my crime comes, I am blazing with hope.
Do me glory, come the whole way across town.

I couldn't rest from hell just anywhere,
in commonplaces, Choiring & strange my pall!
I might not lie still in the waste of St. Paul
or buy DAD's root beer; good signs I forgive.

Drop here, with honour due, my trunk & brain
among the passioning of my countrymen
unable to read, rich proud of their tags
and proud of me. Assemble all my bags!
Bury me in a hole, and give a cheer,
near Cedar on Lake Street, where the used cars live.

*Homage to Mistress Bradstreet, Selections*

17

The winters close, Springs open, no child stirs
under my withering heart, O seasoned heart
God grudged his aid.
All things else soil like a shirt.
Simon is much away. My executive stales.
The town came through for the cartway by the pales,
but my patience is short,
I revolt from, I am like, these savage foresters

18

whose passionless dicker in the shade, whose glance
impassive & scant, belie their murderous cries
when quarry seems to show.
Again I must have been wrong. twice.
Unwell in a new way. Can that begin?
God brandishes. O love. O I love. Kin,
gather. My world is strange
and merciful, ingrown months, blessing a swelling trance.

19

So squeezed. wince you I scream? I love you & hate
off with you. Ages! *Useless.* Below my waist
he has me in Hell's vise.
Stalling. He let go. Come back: brace
me somewhere. No. No. Yes! everything down
hardens I press with horrible joy down
my back cracks like a wrist
shame I am voiding oh behind it is too late

20

hide me forever I work thrust I must free
now I all muscles & bones concentrate

what is living from dying?
Simon I must leave you so untidy
Monster you are killing me Be sure
I'll have you later Women do endure
I can *can* no longer
and it passes the wretched trap whelming and I am me

### 21

drencht & powerful. I did it with my body!
One proud tug greens Heaven. Marvellous.
unforbidding Majesty.
Swell, imperious bells. I fly.
Mountainous, woman not breaks and will bend:
sways God nearby: anguish comes to an end.
Blossomed Sarah, and I
blossom. Is that thing alive? I hear a famisht howl.

### 22

Beloved household. I am Simon's wife.
and the mother of Samuel–whom greedy yet I miss
out of his kicking place.
More in some ways I feel at a loss,
freer. Cantabanks & mummers, nears
longing for you. Our chopping scores my ears.
our costume bores my eyes.
St. George to the good sword. rise! chop-logic's rife
& fever & Satan & Satan's ancient fere.
Pioneering is not feeling well,
not Indians, beasts.
Not all their riddling can forestall
one leaving. Sam, your uncle has had to
go from us to live with God. 'Then Aunt went too?'
Dear, she does wait still.
Stricken: 'Oh. Then he takes us one by one.' My dear.

## 24

Forswearing it otherwise, they starch their minds.
Folkmoots, & blether, blether. John Cotton rakes
to the synod of Cambridge.
Down from my body my legs flow,
out from it arms wave, on it my head shakes.
Now Mistress Hutchinson rings forth a call—
should she? many creep out at a broken wall—
affirming the Holy Ghost
dwells in one justified. Factioning passion blinds

## 25

all to all her good, all—can she be exiled?
Bitter sister, victim! I miss you.
–I miss you, Anne,
day or night weak as a child.
tender & empty, doomed, quick to no tryst.
–I hear you. Be kind, you who leaguer
my image in the mist.
–Be kind you, to one unchained eager far & wild

## 26

and if, O my love, my heart is breaking, please
neglect my cries and I will spare you. Deep
in Time's grave, Love's, you lie still.
Lie still.–Now? That happy shape
my forehead had under my most long, rare,
ravendark, hidden, soft bodiless hair
you award me still.
You must not love me, but I do not bid your cease.

## 27

Veiled my eyes, attending. How can it be I?
Moist, with parted lips, I listen, wicked.

I shake in the morning & retch.
Brood I do on myself naked.
A fading world I dust, with fingers new.
–I have earned the right to be alone with you.
–What right can that be?
Convulsing, if you love, enough, like a sweet lie.

### 28

Not that, I know you can. This cratered skin,
like the crabs & shells of my Palissy ewer, touch!
Oh, you do, you do?
Falls on me what I like a witch,
for lawless holds, annihilations of law
which Time and he and man abhor, foresaw:
sharper than what my Friend
brought me for my revolt when I moved smooth & thin,

### 29

faintings black, rigour, chilling, brown
parching, back, brain burning, the grey pocks
itch, a manic stench
of pustules snapping, pain floods the palm,
sleepless, or a red shaft with a dreadful start
rides at the chapel, like a slipping heart.
My soul strains in one qualm
ah but *this* is not to save me but to throw me down.

### 30

And out of this I lull. It lessens. Kiss me.
That once. As sings out up in sparkling dark
a trail of a star & dies,
while the breath flutters, sounding, mark,
so shorn ought such caresses to us be
who, deserving nothing, flush and flee
the darkness of that light,
a lurching frozen from a warm dream. Talk to me.

## 31

–It is Spring's New England. Pussy willows wedge
up in the wet. Milky crestings, fringed
yellow, in heaven, eyed
by the melting hand-in-hand or mere
desirers single, heavy-footed, rapt,
make surge poor human hearts. Venus is trapt–
the hefty pike shifts, sheer–
in Orion blazing. Warblings, odours, nudge to an edge–

## 32

–Ravishing, ha, what crouches outside ought,
flamboyant, ill, angelic. Often, now,
I am afraid of you.
I am a sobersides; I know.
I *want* to take you for my lover.–Do.
–I hear a madness. Harmless I to you
am not, not I?–No.
–I cannot but be. Sing a concord of our thought.

## 33

–Wan dolls in indigo on gold: refrain
my western lust. I am drowning in this past.
I lose sight of you
who mistress me from air. Unbraced
in delirium of the grand depths, giving away
haunters what kept me, I breathe solid spray.
–I am losing you!
Straiten me on.–I suffered living like a stain:

## 34

I trundle the bodies, on the iron bars,
over that fire backward & forth; they burn;
bits fall. I wonder if

I killed them. Women serve my turn.
–Dreams! You are good.–No.–Dense with hardihood
the wicked are dislodged, and lodged the good.
In green space we are safe.
God awaits us (but I am yielding) who Hell wars.

35

–I cannot feel myself God waits. He flies
nearer a kindly world; or he is flown.
One Saturday's rescue
won't show. Man is entirely alone
may be. I am a man of griefs & fits
trying to be my friend. And the brown smock splits,
down the pale flesh a gash
broadens and Time holds up your heart against my eyes.

36

–Hard and divided heaven! creases me. Shame
is failing. My breath is scented, and I throw
hostile glances towards God.
Crumpling plunge of a pestle, bray:
sin cross & opposite, wherein I survive
nightmares of Eden. Reaches foul & live
he for me, this soul
to crunch, a minute tangle of eternal flame.

37

I fear Hell's hammer-wind. But fear does wane.
Death's blossoms grain my hair; I cannot live.
A black joy clashes
joy, in twilight. The Devil said
'I will deal toward her softly, and her enchanting cries
will fool the horns of Adam.' Father of lies,
a male great pestle smashes
small women swarming towards the mortar's rim in vain.

## 38

I see the cruel spread Wings black with saints!
Silky my breasts not his, mine, mine to withhold
or tender, tender.
I am sifting, nervous, and bold.
The light is changing. Surrender this loveliness
you cannot make me do. *But* I will. Yes.
What horror, down stormy air,
warps towards me? My threatening promise faints

## 39

torture me, Father, lest not I be thine!
Tribunal terrible & pure, my God,
mercy for him and me.
Faces half-fanged, Christ drives abroad,
and though the crop hopes, Jane is so slipshod
I cry. Evil dissolves, & love, like foam;
that love. Prattle of children powers me home,
my heart claps like the swan's
under a frenzy of *who* love me & who shine.

## *The Dream Songs, Selections*

## 1

Huffy Henry hid the day,
unappeasable Henry sulked.
I see his point,–a trying to put things over.
It was the thought that they thought
they could *do* it made Henry wicked & away.
But he should have come out and talked.

All the world like a woolen lover
once did seem on Henry's side.

Then came a departure.
Thereafter nothing fell out as it might or ought.
I don't see how Henry, pried
open for all the world to see, survived.

What he has now to say is a long
wonder the world can bear & be.
Once in a sycamore I was glad
all at the top, and I sang.
Hard on the land wears the strong sea
and empty grows every bed.

5

Henry sats in de bar & was odd,
off in the glass from the glass,
at odds wif de world & its god,
his wife is a complete nothing,
St Stephen
getting even.

Henry sats in de plane & was gay.
Careful Henry nothing said aloud
but where a Virgin out of cloud
to her Mountain dropt in light,
his thought made pockets & the plane buckt.
'Parm me, lady.' 'Orright.'

Henry lay in de netting, wild,
while the brainfever bird did scales;
Mr Heartbreak, the New Man,
come to farm a crazy land;
an image of the dead on the fingernail
of a newborn child.

14

Life, friends, is boring. We must not say so.
After all, the sky flashes, the great sea yearns,

we ourselves flash and yearn,
and moreover my mother told me as a boy
(repeatingly) 'Ever to confess you're bored
means you have no

Inner Resources.' I conclude now I have no
inner resources, because I am heavy bored.
Peoples bore me,
literature bores me, especially great literature,
Henry bores me, with his plights & gripes
as bad as achilles,
who loves people and valiant art, which bores me.
And the tranquil hills, & gin, look like a drag
and somehow a dog
has taken itself & its tail considerably away
into mountains or sea or sky, leaving
behind: me, wag.

15

Let us suppose, valleys & such ago,
one pal unwinding from his labours in
one bar of Chicago,
and this did actual happen. This was so.
And many graces are slipped, & many a sin
even that laid man low

but this will be remembered & told over,
that she was heard at last, haughtful & greasy,
to bawl in that low bar:
'You can biff me, you can bang me, get it you'll never.
I may be only a Polack   broad but I don't lay easy.
Kiss my ass, that's what you are.'

Women is better, braver. In a foehn of loss
entire, which too they hotter understand,
having had it,
we struggle. Some hang heavy on the sauce,
some invest in the past, one hides in the land.
Henry was not his favourite.

## 18

### A Strut for Roethke

Westward, hit a low note, for a roarer lost
across the Sound but north from Bremerton,
hit a way down note.
And never cadenza again of flowers, or cost.
Him who could really do that cleared his throat
& staggered on.

The bluebells, pool-shallows, saluted his over-needs,
while the clouds growled, heh-heh, & snapped, & crashed.

No stunt he'll ever unflinch once more will fail
(O lucky fellow, eh Bones?)—drifted off upstairs,
downstairs, somewheres.
No more daily, trying to hit the head on the nail:
thirstless: without a think in his head:
back from wherever, with it said.

Hit a high long note, for a lover found
needing a lower into friendlier ground
to bug among worms no more
around um jungles where ah blurt 'What for?'
Weeds, too, he favoured as      most men don't favour men.
The Garden Master's gone.

## 22

### Of 1826

I am the little man who smokes & smokes.
I am the girl who does know better but.
I am the king of the pool.
I am so wise I had my mouth sewn shut.
I am a government official & a goddamned fool.
I am a lady who takes jokes.

I am the enemy of the mind.
I am the auto salesman and lóve you.

I am a teenage cancer, with a plan.
I am the blackt-out man.
I am the woman powerful as a zoo.
I am two eyes screwed to my set, whose blind—

It is the Fourth of July.
Collect: while the dying man,
forgone by you creator, who forgives,
is gasping 'Thomas Jefferson still lives'
in vain, in vain, in vain.
I am Henry Pussy-cat! My whiskers fly.

### 75

Turning it over, considering, like a madman
Henry put forth a book.
No harm resulted from this
Neither the menstruating     stars (nor man) was moved
at once.
Bare dogs drew closer for a second look

and performed their friendly operations there.
Refreshed, the bark rejoiced.
Seasons went and came.
Leaves fell, but only a few.
Something remarkable about this
unshedding bulky bole-proud blue-green moist

thing made by savage & thoughtful
surviving Henry
began to strike the passers from despair
so that sore on their shoulders old men hoisted
six-foot sons and polished women called
small girls to dream awhile toward the flashing & bursting
    tree!

76

Henry's Confession

Nothin very bad happen to me lately.
How you explain that?–I explain that, Mr Bones,
terms o' your bafflin odd sobriety.
Sober as man can get, no girls, no telephones,
what could happen bad to Mr Bones?
–*If* life is a handkerchief sandwich,

in a modesty of death I join my father
who dared so long agone leave me.
A bullet on a concrete stoop
clse by a smothering southern sea
spreadeagled on an island, by my knee.
–You is from hunger, Mr Bones,

I offers you this handkerchief, now set
your left foot by my right foot,
shoulder to shoulder, all that jazz,
arm in arm, by the beautiful sea,
hum a little, Mr Bones.
–I saw nobody coming, so I went instead.


121

Grief is fatiguing. He is out of it,
the whole humiliating Human round,
out of this & that.
He made a-many hearts go pit-a-pat
who now need never mind his nostril-hair
nor a critical error laid bare.

He endured fifty years. He was Randall Jarrell
and wrote a-many books & he wrote well.

Peace to the bearded corpse.
His last book was his best. His wives loved him.
He saw in the forest something coming, grim,
but did not change his purpose.

Honest & cruel, peace now to his soul.
He never loved his body, being full of dents.
A wrinkled peace to this good man.
Henry is half in love with one of his students
and the sad process continues to the whole
as it swarmed & began.


149

This world is gradually becoming a place
where I do not care to be any more. Can Delmore die?
I don't suppose
in all them years a day went ever by
without a loving thought for him. Welladay.
In the brightness of his promise,

unstained, I saw him thro' the mist of the actual
blazing with insight, warm with gossip
thro' all our Harvard years
when both of us were just becoming known
I got him out of a police-station once, in Washington, the world is *tref*
and grief too astray for tears.

I imagine you have heard the terrible news,
that Delmore Schwartz is dead, miserably & alone,
in New York: he sang me a song
'I am the Brooklyn poet Delmore Schwartz
Harm & the child I sing, two parents' torts'
when he was young & gift-strong.

162

Henry shuddered: a war which was no war,
the enemy was not our enemy
but theirs whoever they are
and the treaty-end that might conclude it more
unimaginable than *Alice's* third volumn-eee—
and somehow our policy bare

in eighteen costumes kept us unaware
that we were killing Asiatics, daily,
with the disgusting numbers given
on my front page, at which, my love, I stare.
Better would be a definite war with the dragon,
taught to hate us wholly.

Better than the Buddhists self-incinerated
a colossal strike: on military targets
near eighteen Chinese cities.
That would make them think: as we have stated,
an end to aggression will open up new markets
and other quarter-lies.

## OWEN DODSON    [Born 1914]

Owen Dodson was born in New York City. He graduated from Bates College and received a master's degree in fine arts from Yale University. Dodson was a distinguished playwright and novelist as well as poet. He taught drama at Spelman College in Atlanta before moving to Howard University, where he eventually became head of the drama department. In addition to his professional duties, Dodson served as a stage director for many university productions and had plays of his own performed all over the United States. His first volume of verse, *Powerful Long Ladder*, was published in 1946; a notable and more recent effort was 1970's *The Confession Stone: Song Cycles*. His work has appeared widely in magazines and anthologies, and he also authored a libretto for an opera.

### Six O'Clock

I have a river in my mind
Where I have drowned myself
So many times I feel sharp flesh
Of water underneath
My eyelids; and between my toes
The minnows smuggle time
And heard it where all shells begin
To grow what children on the shore
Will beg to listen to.
Horizon, water, land
For me at six o'clock:
A scarlet time of sky
That drinks your rim, horizon;
Turns your blue to blood,
Oh sea; absorbs your green,
Oh land: in scarlet time
I'll see the wave,
The quicksand arm ascend
To master and control
All teeth, death-growing hair,
(Goodbye) Each cell that loves.
(Goodby my dear goodbye)


### Mary Passed This Morning

Letters from Joseph to Martha

i

Martha
Mary passed this morning
funeral this evening     stop
Near six o'clock
tell the others     stop
Raising bus fare for you
stop
          signed Joseph

ii

Dear Martha,
I'm sorry you missed the bus
for the funeral and what not.
I had raised the fare.

to carve some Roman crosses
for a time. When I came back
some years ahead, I courted her;
we were married before Jesus came.
                    signed Joseph

viii

Dear Martha,
I thought Judas had killed himself.
I strolled in the cool gardens
last night to get cool,
to take a stroll.
The darkness was thick
as a wailing wall.
When the moon appeared:
sitting on the wall
under a tree,
smelling a flower,
I saw a man the spit
and image of Judas.
He began to cry at me,
then ran up the hill.
I thought Judas had killed himself!
Burn this letter.
                    signed Joseph

ix

Dear Martha,
I'm glad you have the copy of
the Beatitudes which Jesus wrote

in his own hand. I'm happy Paul
was in your neigborhood.
He tells me you have
rheumatism and arthritis
at the same time . . . (smile)
Walk in the sun
to bake them out.
The weathers here are chancey.
      signed Joseph

                    x

Dear Martha,
I don't write so much now these days:
my hands are getting shaky.
I must be getting old.
I sat at her grave tonight
just to linger there with her.
I wanted to talk with her:
about our life together
and the son. She answered me
in tongues when I whispered
to the grave. I only spoke
the words I knew: 'Mene, mene
teckle uppharsin'.
When I got them out,
she ceased to speak.
What do these words mean?
Oh Martha, answer me. You're wise.
What do these words mean?
What do these words mean?
What did I say?

I'm weary now. I'm tired out.
So I sign my friend to thee,
so I sign my life to her,
so I sign my love to her,
so I sign my love to her.
I must be getting old.

Goodnight, goodnight.
  signed Joseph

Mary didn't look dead
as we took her out to go . . .
Peter began to sing:
'Leaving for home,
leaving for home,
Mary's going home . . .'
I felt like crying,
but I wept. Oh Martha,
Peter kept singing:
'Leaving for home,
going to home,
Mary's almost there . . .'

It was dark twilight
and the sun came out
to go back in again
and hide us all
'leaving for home . . .'

Then John joined Peter:
'Going to home,
Mary's almost there'.
Oh Martha.
     signed Joseph

iii

Dear Martha,
we laid her flat in the earth
where lilies of the valley
and poppies grew with grass;
then there was the laying on
of hands: Peter touched Mary's
face, then the disciples kissed
his hand in equal turn like prayer:
then in equal turn they bowed to me

(Judas was not there)
all the disciples bowed to me.
Mary seemed to smile.
A hallelujah crossed the air.
Some bird began to cry.
I picked some poppies and some lilies:
it was all I could do,
to sprinkle over her.
The bird wept on like a child.
We left her lying there.
Oh oh Martha.

> signed Joseph

iv

Dear Martha,
Mary just finished
baking sesame biscuits
for the poor
before she passed.
Can't find my way clear
to take them out of the oven,
they smell so fresh and good.
Ah Martha . . .

> signed Joseph

v

Dear Martha,
after Mary passed
I carried out her orders:
I dialled her friend
(that I never saw):
his secretary said
he was not in . . .
out somewhere looking
at Sunday for a while.
I thought he should be present
to view the remains and make

remarks. When I called again
she said he was still out there
looking at lilies and the birds.
He should have been in when I called!
  signed Joseph

vi

Dear Martha,
I don't know Lazarus' address
so I am sending these to you.
Mary said Jesus wanted him
to have these garments:
here they are. Tell him
to keep warm and what not.
  signed Joseph

vii

Dear Martha,
you asked how it happened—
from the beginning. Well, when Mary
was sixteen, I noticed her,
then I had to move away


*Sorrow Is the Only Faithful One*

Sorrow is the only faithful one:
The lone companion clinging like a season
To its original skin no matter what the variations.

If all the mountains paraded
Eating the valleys as they went
And the sun were a coiffure on the highest peak,

Sorrow would be there between
The sparkling and the giant laughter
Of the enemy when the clouds come down to swim.

But I am less, unmagic, black,
Sorrow clings to me more than to doomsday mountains
Or erosion scars on a palisade.

Sorrow has a song like a leech
Crying because the sand's blood is dry
And the stars reflected in the lake

Are water for all their twinkling
And bloodless for all their charm.
I have blood, and song.
*Sorrow is the only faithful one.*


### I Break the Sky

Only the deep well
With its reflecting echo
Knows the long dismay
I call this afternoon.

Because my voice is downward
Leaning over shale and torture rock
Surrounding the narrow of this well,
Nothing hears as I cry your name.

There are trees,
The birds they nest are deaf;
All the animals have rejected
The emotion my echo mourns.

Far, far down, the end is prepared
In the sky that breaks as I fall.
I see my face coming, foreshorted descent,
The whiz, the slime–and the sky is whole.

## JEAN GARRIGUE   [Born 1914]

Born in Indiana, Jean Garrigue was for many years associated with the New York poetry scene. Her work was published widely in magazines and anthologies, and, in 1968, an important edition of her work, entitled *New and Selected Poems*, appeared. She taught at Smith College and the University of Pennsylvania as well as serving, for a time, as one of the judges for the National Book Award in poetry. In addition to her poetic endeavors, Garrigue produced works in prose, including a novella, entitled *The Animal Hotel*.

*From Venice Was That Afternoon*

From Venice was that afternoon
Though it was our land's canal we viewed.
There willows clove the bluish heat
By dropping leaf or two, gold green
And every tuft of hill beyond
Stood bright, distinct, as if preserved
By glass that sealed out light but not
Its gold or influence.
And floated on the speckled stream
A child of brilliant innocence
Where on the docks of green we stood
Naming it Love for its perfection.
This seemed to be . . .
But the current carried the leaves swiftly,
So flowed that child away from us,
So stared we sternly at the water's empty face.
Ah, in the greenhouse of that hour
Waited in the tare and sorrel
The mouth of fleshliness that stopped:
The leaves that dappled on that breast
The five-sensed image of our pleasance
Have now destroyed its lineaments.
For the waters of that afternoon
Flowed through Negation's glassy land
Where, in this civil, gate-closed hour
The verges of those waters now

Drown that joy that was our power.
What tyranny imposed this pride
That caused love's gift to be denied
And our destroying features to
Cast perpetually on its brow
The glass accepting no leaves now?
In rages of the intellect
We gave to heaven abstinence
Who said our love must issue from
No cisterns of the ruddy sun
But like the artifice of fountains

Leap from cold, infertile sources.
And our destroying features thus
Cast from that land its beingness
And strewed upon the green-fleshed hills
Sands of our darkening great ills.


*Forest*


There is the star bloom of the moss
And the hairy chunks of light between the conifers;
There are alleys of light where the green leads to a funeral
Down the false floor of needles.
There are rocks and boulders that jut, saw-toothed and urine-yellow.
Other stones in a field look in the distance like sheep grazing,
Grey trunk and trunklike legs and lowered head.
There are short-stemmed forests so close to the ground
You would pity a dog lost there in the spore-budding
Blackness where the sun has never struck down.
There are dying ferns that glow like a gold mine
And weeds and sumac extend the Sodom of color.
Among the divisions of stone and the fissures of branch
Lurk the abashed resentments of the ego.
Do not say this is pleasurable!
Bats, skittering on wires over the lake,
And the bug on the water, bristling in light as he measures forward his
    leaps,
The hills holding back the sun by their notched edges
(What volcanoes lie on the other side
Of heat, light, burning up even the angels)
And the mirror of forests and hills made double,
Do not say this is kindly, convenient,
Warms the hands, crosses the senses with promise,
Harries our fear.
Uneasy, we bellow back at the tree frogs
And, night approaching like the entrance of a tunnel,
We would turn back and cannot, we
Surprise our natures; the woods lock us up
In the secret crimes of our intent.

*Primer of Plato*

All endeavor to be beautiful:
The loved and the loveless as well:
All women rob from duty's time
To pitch adornment to its prime.
The lion in his golden coat
Begets his joy by that; his mate
Beneath that fiery mane repeats
The fury of each sudden sense.
The swan reflecting on the stream
The opposite feathers of the swan-
Webbed dream is like the fox at night
Who glows as in original delight.
Not least, the sun in tedious round
Bestows on rock and land
Principles that all creation
Imitates in adoration.

I never knew this till I
Chanced to see how your bright cheek
Brightened from the gaze of one
Whose spirit swam a Hellespont.
I saw then that beauty was
Both for lover and beloved a feast,
The lover mirroring by his joy
That flush beauty brings, in
His eye her actual face globed small,
And beauty flattered by that glass
Pitched to its highest comeliness,
Doubled and increased until
All would seem
Derived back into first essence.
Both animals and men dwell
In such a mirror of the real
Until in sudden ecstasy
They break the boundaries of that glass
To be the image each first was.

### False Country of the Zoo

We are large with pity, slow and awkward
In the false country of the zoo.
For the beasts our hearts turn over and sigh,
With the gazelle we long to look eye to eye,
Laughter at the stumbling, southern giraffes
Urges our anger, righteous despair.
As the hartebeest plunges, giddy, eccentric,
From out of the courtyard into his stall,
We long to seize his forehead's steep horns
Which are like the staves of a lyre.
Fleeter than greyhounds the hartebeest
Long-muzzled, small-footed, and shy.
Another runner, the emu, is even better
At kicking. Oh, the coarse chicken feet
Of this bird reputed a fossil!
His body, deep as a table,
Droops gracelessly downwise,
His small head shakes like an old woman's eye.
The emu, the ostrich, the cassowary
Continue to go on living their lives
In conditions unnatural to them
And in relations most strange
Remain the same.
As for the secretary bird,
Snake-killer, he suggests
A mischievous bird-maker.
Like a long-legged boy in short pants
He runs teetering, legs far apart,
On his toes, part gasping girl.
What thought him up, this creature
Eminently equipped by his nervous habits
To kill venomous snakes with his strong
Horny feet, first jumping on them
And then leaping away?
At the reptile and monkey houses
Crowds gather to enjoy the ugly
But mock the kangaroo who walks like a cripple.

In the false country of the zoo,
Where Africa is well represented
By Australia,
The emu, the ostrich and cassowary
Survive like kings, poor antiquated strays,
Deceased in all but vestiges,
Who did not have to change, preserved
In their peculiarities by rifts,
From emigration barred.
Now melancholy, like old continents
Unmodified and discontinued, they
Remain by some discreet permission
Like older souls too painfully handicapped.
Running birds who cannot fly,
Whose virtue is their liability,
Whose stubborn very resistance is their sorrow.
See, as they run, how we laugh
At the primitive, relic procedure.

In the false country of the zoo
Grief is well represented there
By those continents of the odd
And outmoded, Africa and Australia.
Sensation is foremost at a zoo—
The sensation of gaping at the particular:
The striped and camouflaged,
The bear, wallowing in his anger,
The humid tiger wading in a pool.
As for those imports
From Java and India,
The pale, virginal peafowl,
The stork, cracking his bill against a wall,
The peacock, plumes up, though he walks as if weighted
—All that unconscionable tapestry—
Till a wind blows the source of his pride
And it becomes his embarrassment,
The eye, plunged in sensation, closes.
Thought seizes the image. This shrieking
Jungle of spot, stripe, orange

Blurs. The oil from the deer's eye
That streaks like a tear his cheek
Seems like a tear, is, is,
As our love and our pity are, are.


### Gravepiece

It is there where the worm has egress
That I prod these bones in their lair
And would push them out of their proper place
To find the vivid core

The heart I pried from the worm's small jaws
When I spied the nail
And its intricate system of holding down the dead
Who weary of the grave's moist hell

Now other than the worm may pulp and tear
For I threw it out of its grinning clothes
It is my heart that runs among these bones
And the virid excess of the enormous hair

In the dead of night the dogs that had the heart
To seize the heart I threw (and rived the air)
Will come with the mangled thing afire on their tongues
And find me out where I stacked the bones

And made a crosstree from the thigh's long ones
Such fire will burst my swound in a shift of bones
Crippled with one for a crutch I will come forth
In the dead of night the dogs will find us both

We will hang on the cross and chatter of love in the winds.

## The Maimed Grasshopper Speaks Up

I have three simple eyes
Perceiving love, death, and hate
Up close, as insects do,
Who thrive by the particular view.

The biggest eyes, with armor on,
That gave me fore and backward sight
Into the ditches of rash thought
Serve me not, the armor's broke.

Thus I may not leap which way
Into the truths of enemy
Or love's fool's ruddy cave
Or the inscrutable world's vault

Lest the rude, simple feelers break.
Thought asks for eyes that see all round
And make its parts to jump the moon,
Monument leapers, leopards of intellect.

Universalists of sight,
I to that moon am like the blind
Who may but feel, not see its light.
And thus in destitution sit.

World without end, commend me to your might
That I my simple eyes may set
On it, or death, or hate, and get some light.


## Lightly Like Music Running

Lightly like music running, our blood
In the darling dogdays of early youth,
We nimbled with vines, ferns were cast over
The limpid lip of the sky, moistness we clambered.
This was the sun come dandling down

Green Babylon in the thronged sheaves—
Shelled such dingles, tan such bloom
By the roved brooksides, all the day long.
Lightly like music running, our blood
In and out of the cloud's woven pastures,
It was all in the shade of the vines and meadows
Where Adam delves, in the green fables
Of the dogdays, in early youth.

### This Day Is Not Like That Day

This day is not like that day.
That was a day majestic with clouds,
Barrows of fruit, ices, and birds,
And in the pink stalls the melon,
While the mango, magniloquent stem,
Steeped him in baskets, Othello's green,
And there were strawberries, the plums and the figs.
This day is not.

That was a day when forth from the farms
The winds, pale as straw, were in mounds
Heaped like green hay freshly torn from ground.
Then did the air thrust so cleanly in leaves
Their delicate fans beat long.
In the water, rings of the sun ran.

And in the skies, the snows
Traveling by feckless shores
Shed forth from their pallid moors
the obscure moon stains of the night
Or those curds of light at the top
From the fissured sides and deep cavern rent
Of the tentless mountains, our guards.

It was a day of gods—sweet provisions
From the wine realm! tournaments!
Castles! our wondering psalms

Bearing up day to its summits day long!
Which now in its dustfall time
Sifts. The attraction
Of stone to stone pulls at the road,
Clouds thin and tear into nothing.

Patience and faith, my heart!
All urns are gathered in dark
With leaves that sang in the sun
Of some rapt mind burning long
In its visions, which vanished.

## DAVID IGNATOW   [Born 1914]

David Ignatow was born in Brooklyn, New York, and lived most of his life in the metropolitan area. He was a businessman for many years but eventually switched to an academic career. As either poet-in-residence or teacher, he was associated with such institutions as Long Island University, Vassar, York College, and the universities of Kansas and Kentucky. He edited the *Beloit Poetry Journal* for a decade and also served as poetry editor for the *Nation* and co-editor of *Chelsea*. He published verse extensively in magazines, including *Poetry*, *Atlantic Monthly*, *The New Yorker*, the *Nation*, and *Commentary*. He was the recipient of the prestigious Shelley Memorial award, the Bollingen Prize for poetry, and an award from the National Institute of Arts and Letters "for a lifetime of creative effort."

### Interior Dialogue

I count the sidewalk slits,
pacing in mind two at a stride.
Therefore, eat your pie before it stales.
But that is dropping the milk!
How shall we feed the babies?
Lots of opinions on that, I'd say.
Just snap your suspenders and wink.
Others might want to grab a hammer.
I'm not for it.
Maybe I'd be, if you dropped me.

I've changed my mind, you see.
Very funny, forgetting in the second verse
that I was not going fast enough in the first.
Don't you drink your coffee that way too?
Of course you do!

Who says?


### Marriage

We are waiting in separate rooms
with doors closed between us.
In the desire to be apart is the wish
to renew ourselves to each other
and so we sit each alone
with nothing to do, really,
for we are all there is to do,
our rooms silent.
                    We listen
to boys in the street
boisterous on a night out.

Our life together has been to shore up good
against evil, to keep us from being flooded apart,

to keep land beneath us: to stem the onrush
of more evil mounting with spite of guilt;
to place a soft wall, evil subsiding against it
in sleep, reproachful sleep that turns
to flowered dreams breathing deeply upon softness
And we have succeeded, by being a wall to each
     other,
to keep us from flooding ourselves with the fiery
and omnivorous.
                    We wave to one another
from the ramparts,
with no man's land between.

You sat across the table and drew pictures,
perhaps of me or of others with us;
you cannot recall, here now bound to me
in marriage. With such mystery is time filled.

I approached from around the table,
smiling, my curiosity to this day
unfilled. What did we do to bring us
together, you smiling at me in return?
A mystery in which we are held
side by side, because it cannot be answered
by a few phrases about love.

I lie here, my thoughts restful
as if life were moving to some haven,
and getting up to find food
for my stomach with the passing hours,
I say, protesting to myself,
But I have lived.


### Epilogue for FDR

How shall we forget your smile
or the bold lift of your arm
or the witticism that pinned your foe?

The first bombs stunned you,
and in the raining shells you grew cool.
We left our farms and cities
to make a phalanx across the land,
closed ranks; and your flowing cape,
once tossed by the wind, lay crushed
between khaki shoulders.

The mourners are marching in uniform
by the millions, thick as lava.
You had spoken of freedom
and man's share in his brother's joy.
We shouldered your beliefs,
lived them by your practical score,
and heard your voice, humorous, direct.
The talents lived for you, the artist
painting hungry faces and a promise;
the writer narrating death
and reporting hope; the dancer
calling up misery and want,
relaxing in love by a body motion;
philosophers, politicians, union men
devising ideas for the fact
and acting upon your good humour,
and insight.

The guns thumping softly in the night,
they were betraying you, pounding holes
in the dark through which air rushed,
escaping, leaving a vacuum for your voice.
We were still, caught each in our separate life,
one with an arm lifted to the sky,
another pointing to earth and to men.
Many were carrying their belongings
or their work in their arms, and all turned,
hearing the air escaped, the guns thumping.
And your voice hardened in the vacuum;
our bodies grew taut; our thoughts,
our lives and work heavy as weapons.

Your casket upon a gun carriage,
we too were still.

Dream of practical love, go by,
drawn by white horses, trained haulers
of guns, our love speaking
to other guns.

### The Poet Is a Hospital Clerk

What I am trying to say is this:
why did I call up the nurse
to chase down the woman visiting her daughter
who had just given birth?
Why did I chase her down?
She had a right to be there,
at the birth of her first grandson.
Couldn't I have let her stay?
Sure I could have let her stay.
Haven't I let others do the same?
Why did I not let her see her grandchild,
when I could feel her feelings?

Because there was a mean canker in me,
a mean streak that comes from bitterness.
From bitterness that comes from disappointment.
From disappointment that comes from frustration.
From frustration that comes from weakness.
From weakness that comes from character.
From character that comes from fears.
From fears that come from cowardice.
From cowardice that comes from a small mind.

And so I let her wait.
And so I made her suffer.
And so I made her feel the way I feel.
I who was looking for fame and glory,
for public leadership, for world acclaim,

for great stature as man and artist,
the greatest yet. Me? Jerk?
Man with nothing to brag about?

I have said it before, I am no good.
I am a jumble of pretense.
I am nonsense shot through with lies and self-
    deception.
Don't I know who I am?
I hold up a mirror to myself and laugh.
What a fool I am.
Do you always fall for the same boasting
and bragging, the same dream of greatness?
Is it not true it never sounds sincere
when you talk of better things to come?
Is it not true you sound more convincing
when you laugh and ridicule yourself,
when you deride and abuse and hate yourself?
Are you not more sure when you talk
of yourself as a failure?

Then you will know what you are talking about.
Laugh at yourself.
You might not even succeed
in talking about yourself as a failure.
You may yet put in the falsest vanities.
You are just a plain no-good failure,
and remember it, just plain.
Why, you even think of writing poetry
at this moment. Don't you realize
the depth of your debasement?

Hate yourself. It might save you.
It might keep you on the level,
having lived in humility and self-distrust.
An ordinary man is a message to the world:
Produce, and be silent.
You may have some dignity in your own eyes,
for you are not being fooled by your small worth.

Do you think you have genius?
Do you think you are entitled to a special consideration?
Have no mercy on yourself.
You are the typical man with illusions of grandeur.
Remember your defeat and be humble.
Take your last rites like a dying man.
In your smallness all that you can do
is to be decent about it.

Show a good front.
Remember, be nice, you pompous fool,
you self-deceiver, you crybaby crab.
Show a good face. March to your death.
In memory of yourself, in sorrow be good to others.
Remember how it hurts to be counted out.
Save that much of your self-respect, your honor,
by being good, you loser.


### Bowery

Bums are the spirit of us parked in ratty old hotels.
Bums are what we have made of angels,
given them old clothes to wear
dirty beards and an alcoholic breath,
to lie sprawled on gutters at our feet
as sacrifices to our idols: power and money.

Bums ask themselves, Why dress and shave,
and be well mannered, studious and hard-working,
own home and debts, a bank account and business
friends when others more eager are doing it
successfully? All we want is the right
to sit propped up against a wall, drunk
and drooling, letting urine seep through
our clothes onto the sidewalk, we
unconscious or unconcerned.
                              We with no money
relax anyway, letting the world come in
on us in sidewalk spit on which we sprawl,

in kicks and jabs from cops, under open skies
in rain and snow. None of you dares do it,
and so you do not know what money means.
We who live on charity enjoy the pleasure
of your wealth, the long hours filled
with drunkenness.

### The Outlaw

They went after him with a long stick,
jabbing into the hole where he had hid himself
in its dark. If he could be forced out
they would shoot him. The stick dug
into his soft parts but he lay there.
It poked hard and he moved aside.
They would fire into the hole
but that it would seem it was they
who had something to worry about.
The woods darkened and they left.
He came slowly from hiding
and in the silence sat up to lift his voice,
to those beyond the woods about to go to bed,
mournful and prolonged.
For that he was despised.

### The Doctor

Entering his office, he looks at his nurse,
hairy, heavy and corseted, nose bulbous,
thick lips that seek the kindness of lipstick.
All of her moves like a ton upon a swinging chain
and as she speaks reminds him of the winds
in the caves of the Pacific shores opening
upon the vacant sea. She speaks, unmarried
to any art or love
and to define herself
moves from desk to his side.

He arrives from a sleepless night of decision
for the ill to whom he has administered his arts
and tricks, all that he has garnered
like fruit with tall reaching or stooping
and patience on one foot, stretching out
for the impossible, to keep alive the dead.

The patient has died. Looking upon the heavy nurse
and the fine bitterness of his longing,
familiar to him as love for which all sacrifice
is just and good and comfortable to one's soul,
for life is us, she approaching him as monolith
to whom life too is given, her tread resounding
on the floor, she makes his human longings
strange to him.

### The Ice Cream Parlor Romance

After malted, licking his lips, he said,
"Let's separate, honey. I'm bored."
And she, the straw sticking to her lips,
looked up at him from her glass.
They had read somewhere that malted was good
for the nerves and anyway there had always been
this corner candy store to go to.
Now moving away from her drink, she said,
"You louse," in just that tone.
It egged him on, he was sure now.
All he wanted was to make her cry.
"I mean it," he said, and she got up
and walked off haughtily. "How about
a piece of chocolate?" he called after her,
throwing down on the table his tip
and the bill money to follow her out—
she disdained to answer—to work on his triumph,
but not before picking up candy
from the counter, with a wave to the storekeeper
that he would pay later.

## THOMAS MERTON   [1915-1968]

Thomas Merton was born in France; his father was an English painter and his mother an American Quaker. After receiving his early education in French and English schools, Merton attended Cambridge University and later, Columbia University. In 1941, three years after his conversion to Catholicism, Merton entered a Trappist monastery near Gethsemani, Kentucky, where he was to spend the rest of his life. Though he concentrated mainly on poetry, translations, and essays, the autobiographical *Seven Storey Mountain* (1948), which focused on his conversion, was a resounding popular success. For many years, Merton lived alone in a cabin on the monastery property. His earlier verse has a distinctly mystical orientation, while the later poems are political and pacifistic in tone.

## *Two British Airmen*

Buried with ceremony in the Teutoburg Forest

Long buried, ancient men-at-arms
Beneath the beechtrees ad the farms
Sleep, and syntax locks their glory
In the old pages of a story.

"We knew that battle when it was
A curious clause in Tacitus,
But were not able to construe
Our graves were in this forest too;
And, buried, never thought to have found
Such strange companions, underground."

"–Bring his flag, and wrap, and lay him
Under a cross that shows no name,
And, in the same ground make his grave
As those long-lost Romans have.
Let him a speechless exile be
From England and his century,
Nor question these old strangers, here,
Inquisitive, around his bier."

Lower, and let the bugle's noise
Supersede the Parson's voice
Who values at too cheap a rate
These men as "servants of their state."
Lower, and let the bombers' noise
Supersede the deacon's voice:
None but perfunctory prayers were said
For the unquiet spirits of these dead.

*The Strife Between the Poet and Ambition*

Money and fame break in the room
And find the poet all alone.
They lock the door, so he won't run,
And turn the radio full-on
And beat the poor dope like a drum.

"Better sing your snatch of song
Before that ostrich voice is dumb,
Better hit your share of gong
Before the sounding brass is mum:
Tomorrow, tomorrow Death will come
And find you sitting dumb and senseless
With your epics unbegun,
And take away your pens and pencils—

There'll be no sculptures on your tomb
And other bards will occupy
Your seven-fifty sitting room."

"Pardon, sirs, my penny face
Bowed to your dollar presences,
Curtsying to Famous Verse,
Flattering wealth with smiles and smirks,
Choking down my hopeless tears!
For someone stole my crate of birds,
And busted up the music box
In which I kept my market flocks
Of bull-ideas and mental bears
And my poetic pocketfox,
My case of literary deers,
My eagle-vans to bat the airs!
They broke the cages and let go
My aviary of metric birds,
And all the diction in my zoo
Was let out by the amateurs!
The fishpond of my Friday words
Is fished out by the days and years.

My whole menagerie of verse
Is ruined by these sly monsieurs!"

The days and years run down the beach
And throw his ideas in the air
And wind his similes up to pitch
And bat his verses out of reach.
He mopes along the empty shore
With gullcries in his windfilled ear.
The hours and minutes, playing catch
With every image they can snatch,
Bat his metaphors to the birds
And cheer him with these bullying words:
"Better sing your snatch of song
Before that ostrich voice is dumb:
Better whack your share of gong
Before the sounding brass is mum:
Tomorrow, tomorrow Death will come
And find your epics unbegun:
There'll be no statues on your tomb,
And other bards will occupy
Your seven-fifty sitting room!"


*Tower of Babel*

The Political Speech

History is a dialogue between
forward and backward
going inevitably forward
by the misuse of words.

Now the function of the word is:
To designate first the machine,
Then what the machine produces
Then what the machine destroys.
Words show us these things not only in order to mean them
But in order to provoke them

And to incorporate us in their forward movement:
Doing, making, destroy or rather
Being done, being made, being destroyed.
Such is history.

The forgotten principle is that the machine
Should always destroy the maker of the machine
Being more important than the maker
Insofar as man is more important than God.
Words also reflect this principle
Though they are meant to conceal it
From the ones who are too young to know.

Thus words have no essential meaning.
They are means of locomotion
From backward to forward
Along an infinite horizontal plane,
Created by the history which they themselves destroy.
They are the makers of our only reality
The backward-forward working of the web
The movement into the web.


### Lent in a Year of War

One of you is a major, made of cord and catskin,

But never dreams his eyes may come to life and thread
The needle-light of famine in a waterglass.

One of you is the paper Jack of Sprites
And will not cast his sentinel voice
Spiraling up the dark ears of the wind
Where the prisoner's yell is lost.

> "What if it was our thumbs put out the sun
> When the Lance and Cross made their mistake?
> You'll never rob us our Eden of drumskin
> shelters,

You, with the bite of John the Baptist's halter,
Getting away in the basket of Paul,
Loving the answer of death, the mother of Lent!"

Thus, in the evening of their sinless murders,
Jack and the Major, sifting the stars for a sign
See the north-south horizon parting like a string!


### Aubade: Lake Erie

When sun, light handed, sows this Indian water
With a crop of cockles,
The vines arrange their tender shadows
In the sweet leafage of an artificial France.

Awake, in the frames of windows, innocent children,
Loving the blue, sprayed leaves of childish life,
Applaud the bearded corn, the bleeding grape,
And cry:
"Here is the hay-colored sun, our marvelous cousin,
Walking in the barley,
Turning the harrowed earth to growing bread,
And spicing the sweet, wounded vine.
Lift up your hitch-hiking heads
And no more fear the fever,
You fugitives, and sleepers in the fields,
Here is the hay-colored sun!"

And when their shining voices, clean as summer,
Play, like churchbells over the field,
A hundred dusty Luthers rise from the dead, unheeding,
Search the horizon for the gap-toothed grin of factories,
And grope, in the green wheat,
Toward the wood winds of the western freight.

### A Psalm

When psalms surprise me with their music
And antiphons turn to rum
The Spirit sings: the bottom drops out of my soul

And from the center of my cellar, Love, louder than thunder
Opens a heaven of naked air.

New eyes awaken.
I send Love's name into the world with wings
And songs grow up around me like a jungle.
Choirs of all creatures sing the tunes
Your Spirit played in Eden.

Zebras and antelopes and birds of paradise
Shine on the face of the abyss
And I am drunk with the great wilderness
Of the sixth day in Genesis.

But sound is never half so fair
As when that music turns to air
And the universe dies of excellence.

Sun, moon and stars
Fall from their heavenly towers.
Joys walk no longer down the blue world's shore.

Though fires loiter, lights still fly on the air of the gulf,
All fear another wind, another thunder:
Then one more voice
Snuffs all their flares in one gust.

And I go forth with no more wine and no more stars
And no more buds and no more Eden
And no more animals and no more sea:
While God sings by Himself in acres of night
And walls fall down, that guarded Paradise.

*St. Malachy*

In November, in the days to remember the dead
When air smells cold as earth,
St. Malachy, who is very old, gets up,
Parts the thin curtain of trees and dawns upon our land.

His coat is filled with drops of rain, and he is bearded
With all the seas of Poseidon.
(Is it a crozier, or a trident in his hand?)
He weeps against the gothic window, and the empty cloister
Mourns like an ocean shell.

Two bells in the steeple
Talk faintly to the old stranger
And the tower considers his waters.
"I have been sent to see my festival," (his cavern speaks!)
"For I am the saint of the day.
Shall I shake the drops from my locks and stand in your
        transept,
Or, leaving you, rest in the silence of my history?"

So the bells rang and we opened the antiphoners
And the wrens and larks flew up out of the pages.
Our thoughts became lambs. Our hearts swam like seas.
One monk believed that we should sing to him
Some stone-age hymn
Or something in the giant language.
So we played to him in the plainsong of the giant Gregory:
Oceans of Scripture sang upon bony Eire.

Then the last salvage of flowers
(Fostered under glass after the gardens foundered)
Held up their little lamps on Malachy's altar
To peer into his wooden eyes before the Mass began.

Rain sighed down the sides of the stone church.
Storms sailed by all day in battle fleets.
At five o'clock, when we tried to see the sun, the
        speechless visitor

Sighed and arose and shook the humus from his feet
And with his trident stirred our trees
And left down-wood, shaking some drops upon the ground

Thus copper flames fall, tongues of fire fall
The leaves in hundreds fall upon his passing
While night sends down her dreadnought darkness
Upon this spurious Pentecost.

And the Melchisedec of our year's end
Who came without a parent, leaves without a trace,
And rain comes rattling down upon our forest
Like the doors of a country jail.

### There Has to Be a Jail for Ladies

There has to be a jail where ladies go
When they are poor, without nice things, and with
    their hair down.
When their beauty is taken from them, when their
    hearts are broken
There is a jail where they must go.

There has to be a jail for ladies, says the Government,
When they are ugly because they are wrong.
It is good for them to stay there a long time
Until the wrong is forgotten.

When no one wants to kiss them any more,
Or only wants to kiss them for money
And take their beauty away
It is right for the wrong to be unheard of for a long
    time
Until the ladies are not remembered.

But I remember one favorite song,
And you ladies may not have forgotten:
"Poor broken blossom, poor faded flower," says my
    song.

Poor ladies, you are jailed roses:
When you speak you curse, when you curse
God and Hell are rusted together in one red voice
Coming as sweet as dust out of a little hollow heart.
Is there no child, then, in that empty heart?

Poor ladies, if you ever sang
It would be brown notes and sad, from understand-
    ing too much
No amount of soapsy sudsy supersuds will make you
Dainty again and not guilty
Until the very end, when you are all forgotten.
There is a jail, where guilt is not forgotten.

Not many days, or many years of that stale wall, that
    smell of disinfectant
Trying, without wanting, to kill your sin
Can make you innocent again:
So I come with this sad song
I love you, dusty and sore,
I love you, unhappy ones.

You are jailed buttercups, you are small field flowers,
To me your voice is not brown
Nor is God rusted together with Hell.
You may curse; but He makes your dry voice turn to
    butter
(Though for the policeman it is still brown)
God becomes your heart's prisoner, He will laugh at
    judges.
He will laugh at the jail.
He will make me write this song.

Keep me in your pocket if you have one. Keep me in
    your heart if you have no pocket.
It is not right for your sorrow to be unknown for-
    ever.
Therefore I come with these voices:

Poor ladies, do not despair—
God will come to your window with skylarks
And pluck each year like a white rose.

## THEODORE WEISS   [Born 1916]

Theodore Weiss was born in Reading, Pennsylvania; he attended Muhlenberg College and Columbia University, where he received his M.A. In subsequent years, he taught variously at the University of North Carolina, Yale, the New School, Bard College, and Princeton. He was a Ford Fellowship winner for the years 1953 to 1954 and received the Wallace Stevens award for his poetry in 1956. Moreover, for many years he edited and published the influential journal, *The Quarterly Review of Literature*.

*The Hook*

I

The students, lost in raucousness,
caught as by the elder Breughel's eye,
we sit in the college store
over sandwiches and coffee, wondering.
She answers eagerly: the place was fine;
sometimes the winds grew very cold,
the snows so deep and wide she lost
sight of people. Yes, she was well
satisfied with her work, expected–
while the quarry's owner was
away–to do another year of it.

II

She is hammering. I hear
the steady sound inside our dry
noisy days. Sparks fly; the mind
so taken is mighty for a moment–
quarry and sculptor both; something
caught like love and war in this
golden mesh: and daring caught
that flings like sparks girls
and boys, flagrant cities prompt
to music's will, love and war
its burly seconds.

III

I see again three kids we passed,
three kids lounging at the edge
of a forsaken quarry like something
they had built; in its sleepy pool
they found the whiteness of their bodies,
the excitement like parian marble.

## IV

Such the waters we find ourselves
in. We sit in the college store absorbed
in food and talk. Eagerness seizes us
like love that leaves its best sailors
in the mighty waves, love the word
for hook whose catching, and the struggle
there, is our deep pleasure. O the sea
is one great musical clash of minds—
each wave a passion and a mind—
a possessed, tumultuous monument
that would be free.

## V

                                    We strain forward
as to some fabulous story. Incandescence
springs from her, the hammer of remembrance
fresh, the young woman, bulky graceful body,
face shining, who sculptured all winter
alone near the source of her rock,
digging down into the difficult rock:
the young woman who lost a day once,
talked to her cat, and when the mirror
of her art became too clear, when dreaming
seemed too big for night alone, took long
walks back to people, back to speech,
and time: the woman who at last—
"I do not use live models"—sculptured fish—
"I remember long lonely holidays at shores
when the spray alone defined green shapes
approaching"—has just seen (her eyes
still gleam with the gleam of it,
blink like the making of many
a take) a great catch.

## VI

April, we say, is the time
for fish, for reaching in the sea-
like air and the outrageousness of growth
one of earth's original conclusions
like the left-over gill slits
the singing student told us about
in this very spot just two days ago . . .
we are in the middle of a great catch,
there collected as from her year-long
lonely rock, the thrashing clean-
scaled, clear-lit shad in the net.

### Cataract

In the falls, music-woven,
clamorous coils as of cymbals
and shields, I see features
purer than my own: desire
lithe and riding, breaker-bearded,
as the wanderer. I see the first
son of my wish whose thews
were tissued of the sea.

And when my hearing tries
the billows of the wind, back
to its snowy crest and back
to its warring mouth, again I meet
the stranger of myself, the one
that sleeps with restlessness
as the distant mutter of drums
the water cores: in jagged fast-
nesses of fire turmoil strides
one with earth's progenitor.

Astonished, I have seen
the rock that moors these seas;

and I am one with the marching
men, possessed as one, their
dazzled minds obeying potions
of the moon–the ragged lair
óf love and hate is one–
the marching men proceeding
by incessant crags, their eyes
reflections of the cataract.

Already gone, the priests
of war, they go to meet them-
selves, to crash into the center
of the drum, the humming waves,
the fiery rocks where
the sirens of the senses
cold, cold O burning cold
calmly thrum the air.

### Preface

*"Sonja Henie," the young girl,*
*looking out of the evening paper,*
*cries, "just got married!"*

*"I don't care if she did,"*
*the mother replies. "She's been*
*married before; it's nothing new."*

Darnel, Ragweed, Wortle

And turning to me, the young poet
tries to say once more what weeds
mean to him–
                luscious weeds
          riding high, wholly personal:
          "O go ahead, hack away as much
          as you like; I've been thrown out
          of better places than this"–

his face just come back from staring
out the window into a day
wandering somewhere in early fall
and a long quiet contented rain,
the sky still on his face, the barn
out there, green-roofed and shiny,
gay in a wet way with its red
wet-streaked sides.
          I read his poem,
mainly about how much it likes weeds,
how definite they are, yet how hard
to come by.
          I say, "Like all the rest
only their own face will do, each
a star squinting through 30,000 years
of storm for its particular sky."

And as though a dream should try
to recollect its dreamer, we look out
across the long highways of rain,
look out.

                 Darnel, Ragweed, Wortle

I do not say what we both are thinking
as we see it flicker in that rain-
soaked day: the face exceeding
face, name, and memory,
yet clinging to our thoughts.
              Black
against the sky, a flock of cranes
shimmers, one unbroken prickly rhythm,
wave on wave, keeping summer jaunty
in its midst.

        *And Sonja Henie,*
*the star, the thin-ice skater,*
*after many tries, tries once more.*

"The poem's not right. I know,
though I worked at it again and again,
I didn't get those old weeds through.
I'm not satisfied, but I'm not done
                with it yet."

There in that wheatfield
of failures, beside all manner
of barns, frost already experimenting,
the slant of weather definitely
fall, lovely scratchy

                                    Darnel, Ragweed, Wortle


*A Certain Village*

Once in late summer,
the road already deep in twilight,
mixing colors with some straggly
wildflowers, I came to a village
I did not know was there

                                    until

I stepped into its narrow street.
Admiring the prim, white houses
nestled among their battered,
lofty trees,
                I found myself in
a tiny square with a little dawdl-
ing fountain and a rickety tower,
its owlish clock absentmindedly
counting minutes now and then.

And in the fountain the face
of morning seemed to linger as
though searching. The air was fresh,
breathing out the fragrances
of a recent shower.

                                    I luxuriated
in my senses, like meeting
unexpectedly a pack of friends
year and years unthought of, laden
with all kinds of gifts.
                         Then
as I stopped to knock at the door
of a house that had seemed occupied
with happy noises, a silence
fell on it,
         the light went out–
and was it instant eyes like flakes,
ten thousand, thousand flakes,
and all unknowing, flurried
round me?
            Wherever I turned
I was met by the unmistakable
accusation, "Stranger!" I, who had,
I thought, begun here and who now
required lodgings
                    for the night,
was denied and from the start.

## ROBERT LOWELL   [1917-1978]

Robert Lowell came from a distinguished line of Bostonian families: the Lowells could look back on generations of judges, historians, and military leaders. The nineteenth century poet James Russell Lowell was a great granduncle, and the Imagist poetess Amy Lowell was a cousin (Robert was actually rather embarrassed by her eccentricities).

In 1937, after two unhappy years at Harvard University (of which another relation had once been president), Robert Lowell transferred to Kenyon College, in order to study with the poet and critic John Crowe Ransom. Through Ransom, he came into contact with Allen Tate and others of the so-called Fugitive movement, who celebrated the peaceful, agricultural society of the South and rejected the frantic, disorienting pace of the industrial Northeast. Lowell further distanced himself from his Protestant New England roots by his 1940 conversion to Catholicism. This led him to oppose U.S. policies in World War II. He declared himself a conscientious objector and spent five months in a New York jail.

Although his first book of poems, *Land of Unlikeness* (1944), did not receive much attention, his second offering, *Lord Weary's Castle* (1946), won the Pulitzer Prize for poetry. Lowell became widely recognized as the foremost younger poet of the period. He achieved an exciting balance between innovation and tradition, injecting power and intensity into conventional forms. With *Life Studies* (1959), however, Lowell's poetry underwent a major change, as the difficult, highly-wrought verse of his early career gave way to a freer, autobiographical poetry. He had been profoundly influenced by the San Francisco Beat movement, spearheaded by Allen Ginsberg, which Lowell experienced firsthand on a reading tour of the west coast. In *Life Studies*, he candidly discusses his marital problems, the several breakdowns he had suffered during the previous decade, and his departure from the Catholic Church. Again, he was lauded by the critics. Subsequent volumes such as *For the Union Dead* (1964), *Notebook* (1969), *For Lizzie and Harriet* (1973), *The Dolphin* (1973), and *Day by Day* (1977) continued in a similar vein. Indeed, so adept was Lowell at this new mode of verse that he became known as "the Leader of the Confessional School."

## The Quaker Graveyard in Nantucket

[For Warren Winslow, Dead At Sea]

*Let man have dominion over the fishes of the sea and the*
*fowls of the air and the beasts of the whole earth, and every*
*creeping creature that moveth upon the earth.*

I

A brackish reach of shoal off Madaket–
The sea was still breaking violently and night
Had steamed into our North Atlantic Fleet,
When the drowned sailor clutched the drag-net. Light
Flashed from his matted head and marble feet,
He grappled at the net
With the coiled, hurdling muscles of his thighs:
The corpse was bloodless, a botch of reds and whites,
Its open, staring eyes
Were lustreless dead-lights
Or cabin-windows on a stranded hulk
Heavy with sand. We weight the body, close
Its eyes and heave it seaward whence it came,
Where the heel-headed dogfish barks its nose
On Ahab's void and forehead; and the name
Is blocked in yellow chalk.
Sailors, who pitch this portent at the sea
Where dreadnaughts shall confess
Its hell-bent deity,
When you are powerless
To sand-bag this Atlantic bulwark, faced
By the earth-shaker, green unwearied, chaste
In his steel scales: ask for no Orphean lute
To pluck life back. The guns of the steeled fleet
Recoil and then repeat
The hoarse salute.

## II

Whenever winds are moving and their breath
Heaves at the roped-in bulwarks of this pier,
The terns and sea-gulls tremble at your death
In these home waters. Sailor, can you hear
The Pequod's sea wings, beating landward, fall
Headlong and break on our Atlantic wall
Off 'Sconset, where the yawing S-boats splash
The bellbuoy, with ballooning spinnakers,
As the entangled, screeching mainsheet clears
The blocks: off Madaket, where lubbers lash
The heavy surf and throw their long lead squids
For blue-fish? Sea-gulls blink their heavy lids
Seaward. The winds' wings beat upon the stones,
Cousin, and scream for you and the claws rush
At the sea's throat and wring it in the slush
Of this old Quaker graveyard where the bones
Cry out in the long night for the hurt beast
Bobbing by Ahab's whaleboats in the East.

## III

All you recovered from Poseidon died
With you, my cousin, and the harrowed brine
Is fruitless on the blue beard of the god,
Stretching beyond us to the castles in Spain,
Nantucket's westward haven. To Cape Cod
Guns, cradled on the tide,
Blast the eelgrass about a waterclock
Of bilge and backwash, roil the salt and sand
Lashing earth's scaffold, rock
Our warships in the hand
Of the great God, where time's contrition blues
Whatever it was these Quaker sailors lost
In the mad scramble of their lives. They died
When time was open-eyed,
Wooden and childish; only bones abide
There, in the nowhere, where their boats were tossed

Sky-high, where mariners had fabled news
Of IS, the whited monster. What it cost
Them is their secret. In the sperm-whale's slick
I see the Quakers drown and hear their cry:
"If God himself had not been on our side,
If God himself had not been on our side,
When the Atlantic rose against us, why,
Then it had swallowed us up quick."

### IV

This is the end of the whaleroad and the whale
Who spewed Nantucket bones on the thrashed swell
And stirred the troubled waters to whirlpools
To send the Pequod packing off to hell:
This is the end of them, three-quarters fools,
Snatching at straws to sail
Seaward and seaward on the turntail whale,
Spouting out blood and water as it rolls,
Sick as a dog to these Atlantic shoals:
*Clamavimus*, O depths. Let the sea-gulls wail

For water, for the deep where the high tide
Mutters to its hurt self, mutters and ebbs.
Waves wallow in their wash, go out and out,
Leave only the death-rattle of the crabs,
The beach increasing, its enormous snout
Sucking the ocean's side.
This is the end of running on the waves;
We are poured out like water. Who will dance
The mast-lashed master of Leviathans
Up from this field of Quakers in unstoned graves?

### V

When the whale's viscera go and the roll
Of its corruption overruns this world
Beyond tree-swept Nantucket and Woods Hole
And Martha's Vineyard, Sailor, will your sword

Whistle and fall and sink into the fat?
In the great ash-pit of Jehoshaphat
The bones cry for the blood of the white whale,
The fat flukes arch and whack about its ears,
The death-lance churns into the sanctuary, tears
The gun-blue swingle, heaving like a flail,
And hacks the coiling life out: it works and drags
And rips the sperm-whale's midriff into rags,
Gobbets of blubber spill to wind and weather,
Sailor, and gulls go round the stoven timbers
Where the morning stars sing out together
And thunder shakes the white surf and dismembers
The red flag hammered in the mast-head. Hide,
Our steel, Jonas Messias, in Thy side.

## VI

### Our Lady Of Walsingham

There once the penitents took off their shoes
And then walked barefoot the remaining mile;
And the small trees, a stream and hedgerows file
Slowly along the munching English lane,
Like cows to the old shrine, until you lose
Track of your dragging pain.
The stream flows down under the druid tree,
Shiloah's whirlpools gurgle and make glad
The castle of God. Sailor, you were glad
And whistled Sion by that stream. But see:

Our Lady, too small for her canopy,
Sits near the altar. There's no comeliness
At all or charm in that expressionless
Face with its heavy eyelids. As before,
This face, for centuries a memory,
*Non est species, neque decor,*
Expressionless, expresses God: it goes
Past castled Sion. She knows what God knows,

Not Calvary's Cross nor crib at Bethlehem
Now, and the world shall come to Walsingham.

## VII

The empty winds are creaking and the oak
Splatters and splatters on the cenotaph,
The boughs are trembling and a gaff
Bobs on the untimely stroke
Of the greased wash exploding on a shoal-bell
In the old mouth of the Atlantic. It's well;
Atlantic, you are fouled with the blue sailors,
Sea-monsters, upward angel, downward fish:
Unmarried and corroding, spare of flesh
Mart once of supercilious, wing'd clippers,
Atlantic, where your bell-trap guts its spoil
You could cut the brackish winds with a knife
Here in Nantucket, and cast up the time
When the Lord God formed man from the sea's slime
And breathed into his face the breath of life,
And blue-lung'd combers lumbered to the kill.
The Lord survives the rainbow of His will.

### The Drunken Fisherman

Wallowing in this bloody sty,
I cast for fish that pleased my eye
(Truly Jehovah's bow suspends
No pots of gold to weight its ends);
Only the blood-mouthed rainbow trout
Rose to my bait. They flopped about
My canvas creel until the moth
Corrupted its unstable cloth.

A calendar to tell the day;
A handkerchief to wave away
The gnats; a couch unstuffed with storm

Pouching a bottle full of worms;
And bedroom slacks: are these fit terms
To mete the worm whose molten rage
Boils in the belly of old age?

Once fishing was a rabbit's foot—
O wind blow cold, O wind blow hot,
Let suns stay in or suns step out:
Life danced a jig on the sperm-whale's spout—
The fisher's fluent and obscene
Catches kept his conscience clean.
Children, the raging memory drools
Over the glory of past pools.

Now the hot river, ebbing, hauls
Its bloody waters into holes;
A grain of sand inside my shoe
Mimics the moon that might undo
Man and Creation too; remorse,
Stinking, has puddled up its source;
Here tantrums thrash to a whale's rage.
This is the pot-hole of old age.

Is there no way to cast my hook
Out of this dynamited brook?
The Fisher's sons must cast about
When shallow waters peter out.
I will catch Christ with a greased worm,
And when the Prince of Darkness stalks
My bloodstream to its Stygian term . . .
On water the Man-Fisher walks.

## At the Indian Killer's Grave

*"Here, also, are the veterans of King Philip's War, who
burned villages and slaughtered young and old, with pious
fierceness, while the godly souls throughout the land were
helping them with prayer."*

HAWTHORNE

Behind King's Chapel what the earth has kept
Whole from the jerking noose of time extends
Its dark enigma to Jehoshaphat;
Or will King Philip plait
The just man's scalp in the wailing valley! Friends,
Blacker than these black stones the subway bends
About the dirty elm roots and the well
For the unchristened infants in the waste
Of the great garden rotten to its root;
Death, the engraver, puts forward his bone foot
And Grace-with-wings and Time-on-wings compel
All this antique abandon of the disgraced
To face Jehovah's buffets and his ends.

The dusty leaves and frizzled lilacs gear
This garden of the elders with baroque
And prodigal embellishments but smoke,
Settling upon the pilgrims and their grounds,
Espouses and confounds
Their dust with the off-scourings of the town;
The libertarian crown
Of England built their mausoleum. Here
A clutter of Bible and weeping willows guards
The stern Colonial magistrates and wards
Of Charles the Second, and the clouds
Weep on the just and unjust as they will—
For the poor dead cannot see Easter crowds
On Boston Common or the Beacon Hill
Where strangers hold the golden Statehouse dome
For good and always. Where they live is home:

A common with an iron railing: here
Frayed cables wreathe the spreading cenotaph
Of John and Mary Winslow and the laugh
Of Death is hacked in sandstone, in their year.

A green train grinds along its buried tracks
And screeches. When the great mutation racks
The Pilgrim Father's relics, will these plaques
Harness the spare-ribbed persons of the dead
To battle with the dragon? Philip's head
Grins on the platter, fouls in pantomime
The fingers of kept time:
"Surely, this people is but grass,"
He whispers, "this will pass;
But, Sirs, the trollop dances on your skulls
And breaks the hollow noddle like an egg
That thought the world an eggshell. Sirs, the gulls
Scream from the squelching wharf-piles, beg a leg
To crack their crops. The Judgment is at hand;
Only the dead are poorer in this world
Where State and elders thundered *raca*, hurled
Anathemas at nature and the land
That fed the hunter's gashed and green perfection—
Its settled mass concedes no outlets for your puns
And verbal Paradises. Your election,
Hawking above this slime
For souls as single as their skeletons,
Flutters and claws in the dead hand of time."

When you go down this man-hole to the drains,
The doorman barricades you in and out;
You wait upon his pleasure. All about
The pale, sand-colored, treeless chains
Of T-squared buildings strain
To curb the spreading of the braced terrain;
When you go down this hole, perhaps your pains
Will be rewarded well; no rough-cast house
Will bed and board you in King's Chapel. Here
A public servant putters with a knife

And paints the railing red
Forever, as a mouse
Cracks walnuts by the headstones of the dead
Whose chiseled angels peer
At you, as if their art were long as life.

I ponder on the railing at this park:
Who was the man who sowed the dragon's teeth,
That fabulous or fancied patriarch
Who sowed so ill for his descent, beneath
King's Chapel in this underworld and dark?
John, Matthew, Luke and Mark,
Gospel me to the Garden, let me come
Where Mary twists the warlock with her flowers—
Her soul a bridal chamber fresh with flowers
And her whole body an ecstatic womb,
As through the trellis peers the sudden Bridegroom.

### After the Surprising Conversions

*September twenty-second,* Sir: today
I answer. In the latter part of May,
Hard on our Lord's Ascension, it began
To be more sensible. A gentleman
Of more than common understanding, strict
In morals, pious in behavior, kicked
Against our goad. A man of some renown,
An useful, honored person in the town,
He came of melancholy parents; prone
To secret spells, for years they kept alone—
His uncle, I believe, was killed of it:
Good people, but of too much or little wit.
I preached one Sabbath on a text from Kings;
He showed concernment for his soul. Some things
In his experience were hopeful. He
Would sit and watch the wind knocking a tree
And praise this countryside our Lord has made.
Once when a poor man's heifer died, he laid

A shilling on the doorsill; though a thirst
For loving shook him like a snake, he durst
Not entertain much hope of his estate
In heaven. Once we saw him sitting late
Behind his attic window by a light
That guttered on his Bible; through that night
He meditated terror, and he seemed
Beyond advice or reason, for he dreamed
That he was called to trumpet Judgment Day
To Concord. In the latter part of May
He cut his throat. And though the coroner
Judged him delirious, soon a noisome stir
Palsied our village. At Jehovah's nod
Satan seemed more let loose amongst us: God
Abandoned us to Satan, and he pressed
Us hard, until we thought we could not rest
Till we had done with life. Content was gone.
All the good work was quashed. We were undone.
The breath of God had carried out a planned
And sensible withdrawal from this land;
The multitude, once unconcerned with doubt,
Once neither callous, curious nor devout,
Jumped at broad noon, as though some peddler groaned
At it in its familiar twang: "My friend,
Cut your own throat. Cut your own throat. Now! Now!"
September twenty-second, Sir, the bough
Cracks with the unpicked apples, and at dawn
The small-mouth bass breaks water, gorged with spawn.


### Where the Rainbow Ends

I saw the sky descending, black and white,
Not blue, on Boston where the winters wore
The skulls to jack-o'-lanterns on the slates,
And Hunger's skin-and-bone retrievers tore
The chickadee and shrike. The thorn tree waits
Its victim and tonight
The worms will eat the deadwood to the foot

Of Ararat: the scythers, Time and Death,
Helmed locusts, move upon the tree of breath;
The wild ingrafted olive and the root

Are withered, and a winter drifts to where
The Pepperpot, ironic rainbow, spans
Charles River and its scales of scorched-earth miles.
I saw my city in the Scales, the pans
Of judgment rising and descending. Piles
Of dead leaves char the air—
And I am a red arrow on this graph
Of Revelations. Every dove is sold
The Chapel's sharp-shinned eagle shifts its hold
On serpent-Time, the rainbow's epitaph.

In Boston serpents whistle at the cold.
The victim climbs the altar steps and sings:
"Hosannah to the lion, lamb, and beast
Who fans the furnace-face of IS with wings:
I breathe the ether of my marriage feast."
At the high altar, gold
And a fair cloth, I kneel and the wings beat
My cheek. What can the dove of Jesus give
You now but wisdom, exile? Stand and live,
The dove has brought an olive branch to eat.


*To Delmore Schwartz*

Cambridge 1946

We couldn't even keep the furnace lit!
Even when we had disconnected it,
the antiquated
refrigerator gurgled mustard gas
through your mustard-yellow house,
and spoiled our long maneuvered visit
from. T.S. Eliot's brother, Henry Ware. . . .

Your stuffed duck craned toward Harvard from my trunk:
its bill was a black whistle, and its brow
was high and thinner than a baby's thumb;
its webs were tough as toenails on its bough.
It was your first kill; you had rushed it home,
pickled in a tin wastebasket of rum—
it looked through us, as if it'd died dead drunk.
You must have propped its eyelids with a nail,
and yet it lived with us and met our stare,
Rabelaisian, lubricious, drugged. And there,
perched on my trunk and typing-table,
it cooled our universal
*Angst* a moment, Delmore. We drank and eyed
the chicken-hearted shadows of the world.
Underseas fellows, nobly mad,
we talked away our friends. "Let Joyce and Freud,
the Masters of Joy,
be our guests here," you said. The room was filled
with cigarette smoke circling the paranoid,
inert gaze of Coleridge, back
from Malta—his eyes lost in flesh, lips baked and black.
Your tiger kitten, *Oranges*,
cartwheeled for joy in a ball of snarls.
You said:
*"We poets in our youth begin in sadness;*
*thereof in the end come despondency and madness;*
Stalin has had two cerebral hemorrhages!"
The Charles
River was turning silver. In the ebb-
light of morning, we stuck
the duck
-'s web-
foot, like a candle, in a quart of gin we'd killed.

I

*My Last Afternoon*
*with Uncle Devereux Winslow*

1922: the stone porch of my Grandfather's summer house

I

"I won't go with you. I want to stay with Grandpa!"
That's how I threw cold water
on my Mother and Father's
watery martini pipe dreams at Sunday dinner.
. . . Fontainebleau, Mattapoisett, Puget Sound . . . .
Nowhere was anywhere after a summer
at my Grandfather's farm.
Diamond-pointed, athirst and Norman,
its alley of poplars
paraded from Grandmother's rose garden
to a scary stand of virgin pine,
scrub, and paths forever pioneering.

One afternoon in 1922,
I sat on the stone porch, looking through
screens as black-grained as drifting coal.
*Tockytock, tockytock*
clumped our Alpine, Edwardian cuckoo clock,
slung with strangled, wooden game.
Our farmer was cementing a root-house under the hill.
One of my hands was cool on a pile
of black earth, the other warm
on a pile of lime. All about me
were the works of my Grandfather's hands:
snapshots of his *Liberty Bell* silver mine;
his high school at *Stuttgart am Neckar*;
stogie-brown beams; fools'-gold nuggets;
octagonal red tiles,
sweaty with a secret dank, crummy with ant-stale;

a Rocky Mountain chaise longue,
its legs, shellacked saplings.
A pastel-pale Huckleberry Finn
fished with a broom straw in a basin
hollowed out of a millstone.
Like my Grandfather, the décor
was manly, comfortable,
overbearing, disproportioned.

What were those sunflowers? Pumpkins floating shoulder-high?

It was sunset, Sadie and Nellie
bearing pitchers of ice-tea,
oranges, lemons, mint, and peppermints,
and the jug of shandygaff,
which Grandpa made by blending half and half
yeasty, wheezing homemade sarsaparilla with beer.
The farm, entitled *Char-de-sa*
in the Social Register,
was named for my Grandfather's children:
Charlotte, Devereux, and Sarah.
No one had died there in my lifetime . . .
Only Cinder, our Scottie puppy
paralyzed from gobbling toads.
I sat mixing black earth and lime.

II

I was five and a half.
My formal pearl gray shorts
had been worn for three minutes.
My protection was the Olympian
poise of my models in the imperishable autumn
display windows
of Rogers Pett's boys' store below the State House
in Boston. Distorting drops of water
pinpricked my face in the basin's mirror.
I was a stuffed toucan
with a bibulous, multicolored beak.

### III

Up in the air
by the lakeview window in the billiards-room,
lurid in the doldrums of the sunset hour,
my Great Aunt Sarah
was learning *Samson and Delilah.*
She thundered on the keyboard of her dummy piano,
with gauze curtains like a boudoir table,
accordionlike yet soundless.
It had been bought to spare the nerves
of my Grandmother,
tone-deaf, quick as a cricket,
now needing a fourth for "Auction,"
and casting a thirsty eye
on Aunt Sarah, risen like the phoenix
from her bed of troublesome snacks and Tauchnitz classics.

Forty years earlier,
twenty, auburn headed,
grasshopper notes of genius!
Family gossip says Aunt Sarah
tilted her archaic Athenian nose
and jilted an Astor.
Each morning she practiced
on the grand piano at Symphony Hall,
deathlike in the off-season summer—
its naked Greek statues draped with purple
like the saints in Holy Week. . . .
On the recital day, she failed to appear.

### IV

I picked with a clean finger nail at the blue anchor
on my sailor blouse washed white as a spinnaker.
What in the world was I wishing?
. . . A sail-colored horse browsing in the bullrushes . . .
A fluff of the west wind puffing
my blouse, kiting me over our seven chimneys,

troubling the waters. . . .
As small as sapphires were the ponds: *Quittacus, Snippituit,*
and *Assawompset,* halved by "the Island,"
where my Uncle's duck blind
floated in a barrage of smoke-clouds.
Double-barreled shotguns
stuck out like bundles of baby crow-bars.
A single sculler in a camouflaged kayak
was quacking to the decoys. . . .

At the cabin between the waters,
the nearest windows were already boarded.
Uncle Devereux was closing camp for the winter.
As if posed for "the engagement photograph,"
he was wearing his severe
war-uniform of a volunteer Canadian officer.
Daylight from the doorway riddled his student posters,
tacked helter-skelter on walls as raw as a boardwalk.
Mr. Punch, a water melon in hockey tights,
was tossing off a decanter of Scotch.
*La Belle France* in a red, white and blue toga
was accepting the arm of her "protector,"
the intu and porcine Edward VII.
The pre-war music hall belles
had goose necks, glorious signatures, beauty-moles,
and coils of hair like rooster tails.
The fines poster was two or three young men in khaki kilts
being bushwhacked on the veldt–
they were almost life-size. . . .

My Uncle was dying at twenty-nine.
"You are behaving like children,"
said my Grandfather,
when my Uncle and Aunt left their three baby daughters,
and sailed for Europe on a last honeymoon . . .
I cowered in terror.
I wasn't a child at all–
unseen and all-seeing, I was Agrippina
in the Golden House of Nero. . . .

Near me was the white measuring-door
my Grandfather had penciled with my Uncle's heights.
In 1911, he had stopped growing at just six feet.
While I sat on the tiles,
and dug at the anchor on my sailor blouse,
Uncle Devereux stood behind me.
He was as brushed as Bayard, our riding horse.
His face was putty.
His blue coat and white trousers
grew sharper and straighter.
His coat was a blue jay's tail,
his trousers were solid cream from the top of the bottle.
He was animated, hierarchical,
like a ginger snap man in a clothes-press.
He was dying of the incurable Hodgkin's disease. . . .
My hands were warm, then cool, on the piles
of earth and lime,
a black pile and a white pile. . . .
Come winter,
Uncle Devereux would blend to the one color.


*Father's Bedroom*


In my Father's bedroom:
blue threads as thin
as pen-writing on the bedspread,
blue dots on the curtains,
a blue kimono,
Chinese sandals with blue plush straps.
The broad-planked floor
had a sandpapered neatness.
The clear glass bed-lamp
with a white doily shade
was still raised a few
inches by resting on volume two
of Lafcadio Hearn's
*Glimpses of Unfamiliar Japan.*
Its warped olive cover

was punished like a rhinoceros hide.
In the flyleaf:
"Robbie from Mother."
Years later in the same hand:
"This book has had hard usage
on the Yangtze River, China.
It was left under an open
porthole in a storm."

## GWENDOLYN BROOKS   [Born 1917]

Gwendolyn Brooks was born in Topeka, Kansas, but grew up in Chicago, where, as an adult, she became deeply involved with the problems and challenges facing the poor Black community. She began writing while still a child, compiling poetry notebooks at the age of eleven. She attended the Englewood High School in Chicago and graduated from Wilson Junior College. Her first published poems appeared in *Poetry* magazine when she was twenty-eight; soon thereafter, her first volume of poems, *A Street in Bronzeville* (1945), was released. (Bronzeville was the Black ghetto of Chicago.) Four years later, with her second book, *Annie Allen* (1949), Brooks became the first Black ever to receive the Pulitzer Prize for poetry. A turning point in her career came at the Second Black Writer's Conference, held at Fisk University in 1967. While her work had always offered a vivid, unsentimentalized portrait of urban Black life, it now acquired a harder, politicized edge. Inspired by the young poets she met at the Conference, Brooks became convinced of the necessity of writing specifically for a Black audience. Consistent with this change was her decision thenceforward to have her work printed by Black publishers, such as the Broadside Press.

*A Street in Bronzeville*

to David and Keziah Brooks

kitchenette building

We are things of dry hours and the involuntary plan,
Grayed in, and gray. "Dream" makes a giddy sound, not
        strong
Like "rent," "feeding a wife," "satisfying a man."

But could a dream send up through onion fumes
Its white and violet, fight with fried potatoes
And yesterday's garbage ripening in the hall,
Flutter, or sing an aria down these rooms

Even if we were willing to let it in,
Had time to warm it, keep it very clean,
Anticipate a message, let it begin?

We wonder. But not well! not for a minute!
Since Number Five is out of the bathroom now,
We think of lukewarm water, hope to get in it.


the mother

Abortions will not let you forget.
You remember the children you got that you did not get,
The damp small pulps with a little or with no hair,
The singers and workers that never handled the air.
You will never neglect or beat
Them, or silence or buy with a sweet.
You will never wind up the sucking-thumb
Or scuttle off ghosts that come.
You will never leave them, controlling your luscious sigh,
Return for a snack of them, with gobbling mother-eye.

I have heard in the voices of the wind the voices of my dim
     killed children.
I have contracted. I have eased
My dim dears at the breasts they could never suck.
I have said, Sweets, if I sinned, if I seized
Your luck
And your lives from your unfinished reach,
If I stole your births and your names,
Your straight baby tears and your games,
Your stilted or lovely loves, your tumults, your marriages,
          aches, and your deaths,
If I poisoned the beginnings of your breaths,
Believe that even in my deliberateness I was not deliberate.
Though why should I whine,
Whine that the crime was other than mine?–
Since anyhow you are dead.
Or rather, or instead,
You were never made.
But that too, I am afraid,
Is faulty: oh, what shall I say, how is the truth to be said?
You were born, you had body, you died.
It is just that you never giggled or planned or cried.

Believe me, I loved you all.
Believe me, I knew you, though faintly, and I loved, I loved you
All.


                    southeast corner

The School of Beauty's a tavern now.
The Madam is underground.
Out a Lincoln, among the graves
Her own is early found.
Where the thickest, tallest monument
Cuts grandly into the air
The Madam lies, contentedly.
Her fortune, too, lies there,

Converted into cool hard steel
And right red velvet lining;
While over her tan impassivity
Shot silk is shining.


### hunchback girl: she thinks of heaven

My Father, it is surely a blue place
And straight. Right. Regular. Where I shall find
No need for scholarly nonchalance or looks
A little to the left or guards upon the
Heart to halt love that runs without crookedness
Along its crooked corridors. My Father,
It is a planned place surely. Out of coils,
Unscrewed, released, no more to be marvelous,
I shall walk straightly through most proper halls
Proper myself, princess of properness.


### a song in the front yard

I've stayed in the front yard all my life.
I want a peek at the back
Where it's rough and untended and hungry weed grows.
A girl gets sick of a rose.

I want to go in the back yard now
And maybe down the alley,
To where the charity children play.
I want a good time today.

They do some wonderful things.
They have some wonderful fun.
My mother sneers, but I say it's fine
How they don't have to go in at quarter to nine.
My mother, she tells me that Johnnie Mae
Will grow up to be a bad woman.
That George'll be taken to Jail soon or late

(On account of last winter he sold our back gate).

But I say it's fine. Honest, I do.
And I'd like to be a bad woman, too,
And wear the brave stockings of night-black lace
And strut down the streets with paint on my face.


the ballad of chocolate Mabbie

It was Mabbie without the grammar school gates.
And Mabbie was all of seven.
And Mabbie was cut from a chocloate bar.
And Mabbie thought life was heaven.

The grammar school gates were the pearly gates,
For Willie Boone went to school.
When she sat by him in history class
Was only her eyes were cool.

It was Mabbie without the grammar school gates.
Waiting for Willie Boone.
Half hour after the closing bell!
He would surely be coming soon.

Oh, warm is the waiting for joys, my dears!
And it cannot be too long.
Oh, pity the little poor chocolate lips
That carry the bubble of song!

Out came the saucily bold Willie Boone.
It was woe for our Mabbie now.
He wore like a jewel a lemon-hued lynx
With sand-waves loving her brow.

It was Mabbie alone by the grammar school gates.
Yet chocolate companions had she:
Mabbie on Mabbie with hush in the heart.
Mabbie on Mabbie to be.

the preacher: ruminates behind the sermon

I think it must be lonely to be God.
Nobody loves a master. No. Despite
The bright hosannas, bright dear-Lords, and bright
Determined reverence of Sunday eyes.

Picture Jehovah striding through the hall
Of His importance, creatures running out
From servant-corners to acclaim, to shout
Appreciation of His merit's glare.

But who walks with Him?–dares to take His arm,
To slap Him on the shoulder, tweak His ear,
Buy Him a Coca-Cola or a beer,
Pooh-pooh His politics, call Him a fool?

Perhaps–who knows?–He tires of looking down.
Those eyes are never lifted. Never straight.
Perhaps sometimes He tires of being great
In solitude. Without a hand to hold.


Sadie and Maud

Maud went to college.
Sadie stayed at home.
Sadie scraped life
With a fine-tooth comb.

She didn't leave a tangle in.
Her comb found every strand.
Sadie was one of the livingest chits
In all the land.

Sadie bore two babies
Under her maiden name.
Maud and Ma and Papa
Nearly died of shame.

When Sadie said her last so-long
Her girls struck out from home.
(Sadie had left a heritage
Her fine-tooth comb.)

Maud, who went to college,
Is a thin brown mouse.
She is living all alone
In this old house.

### the independent man

Now who could take you off to tiny life
In one room or in two rooms or in three
And cork you smartly, like the flask of wine
You are? Not any woman. Not a wife.
You'd let her twirl you, give her a good glee
Showing your leaping ruby to a friend.
Though twirling would be meek. Since not a cork
Could you allow, for being made so free.

A woman would be wise to think it well
If once week you only rang the bell.

### of De Witt Williams on his way to Lincoln Cemetery

He was born in Alabama.
He was bred in Illinois.
He was nothing but a
Plain black boy.

Swing low swing low sweet sweet chariot.
Nothing but a plain black boy.

Drive him past the Pool Hall.
Drive him past the Show.
Blind within his casket,
But maybe he will know.

Down through Forty-seventh Street:
Underneath the L,
And Northwest Corner, Prairie,
That he loved so well.

Don't forget the Dance Halls—
Warwick and Savoy,
Where he picked his women, where
He drank his liquid joy.

Born in Alabama.
Bred in Illinois.
He was nothing but a
Plain black boy.

Swing low swing low sweet sweet chariot.
Nothing but a plain black boy.


the vacant lot

Mrs. Coley's three-flat brick
Isn't here any more.
All done with seeing her fat little form
Burst out of the basement door;
And with seeing her Afican son-in-law
(Rightful heir to the throne)
With his great white strong cold squares of teeth
And his little eyes of stone;
And with seeing the squat fat daughter
Letting in the men
When majesty has gone for the day—
And letting them out again.

*Negro Hero*

to suggest Dorie Miller

I had to kick their law into their teeth in order to save them.
However I have heard that sometimes you have to deal
Devilishly with drowning men in order to swim them to shore.
Or they will haul them selves and you to the trash and the fish
        beneath.
(When I think of this, I do not worry about a few
Chipped teeth.)

It is good I gave glory, it is good I put gold on their name.
Or there would have been spikes in the afterward hands.
But let us speak only of my success and the pictures in the
        Caucasian dailies
As well as the Negro weeklies. For I am a gem.
(They are not concerned that it was hardly The Enemy my
        fight was against
But them.)

It was a tall time. And of course my blood was
Boiling about in my head and straining and howling and
        singing me on.
Of course I was rolled on wheels of my boy itch to get at
        the gun.
Of course all the delicate rehearsal shots of my childhood
        massed in mirage before me.
Of course I was child
And my first swallow of the liquor of battle bleeding black
        air dying and demon noise
Made me wild.

It was kinder than that, though, and I showed like a banner
        my kindness.
I loved. And a man will guard when he loves.
Their white-gowned democracy was my fair lady.
With her knife lying cold, straight, in the softness of her
        sweet-flowing sleeve.

But for the sake of the dear smiling mouth and the stuttered
      promise I toyed with my life.
I threw back!–I would not remember
Entirely the knife.

Still–am I good enough to die for them, is my blood bright
      enough to be spilled,
Was my constant back-question–are they clear
On this? Or do I intrude even now?
Am I clean enough to kill for them, do they wish me to kill
For them or is my place while death licks his lips and strides
      to them
In the galley still?

(In a southern city a white man said
Indeed, I'd rather be dead;
Indeed, I'd rather be shot in the head
Or ridden to waste on the back of a flood
Than saved by the drop of a black man's blood.)

Naturally, the important thing is, I helped to save them, them
      and a part of their democracy.
Even if I had to kick their law into their teeth in order to
      do that for them.
And I am feeling well and settled in myself because I believe
      it was a good job,
Despite this possible horror: that they might prefer the
Preservation of their law in all its sick dignity and their
      knives
To the continuation of their creed
And their lives.

*The Lovers of the Poor*

               arrive. The Ladies from the Ladies' Betterment
       League
Arrive in the afternoon, the late light slanting
In diluted gold bars across the boulevard brag
Of proud, seamed faces with mercy and murder hinting
Here, there, interrupting, all deep and debonair,
The pink paint on the innocence of fear;
Walk in a gingerly manner up the hall.
Cutting with knives served by their softest care,
Served by their love, so barbarously fair.
Whose mothers taught: You'd better not be cruel!
You had better not throw stones upon the wrens!
Herein they kiss and coddle and assault
Anew and dearly in the innocence
With which they baffle nature. Who are full,
Sleek, tender-clad, fit, fiftyish, a-glow, all
Sweetly abortive, hinting at fat fruit,
Judge it high time that fiftyish fingers felt
Beneath the lovelier planes of enterprise.
To resurrect. To moisten with milky chill.
To be a random hitching-post or plush.
To be, for wet eyes, random and handy hem.
               Their guild is giving money to the poor.
The worthy poor. The very very worthy
And beautiful poor. Perhaps just not too swarthy?
Perhaps just not too dirty nor too dim
Nor–passionate. In truth, what they could wish
Is–something less than derelict or dull.
Not staunch enough to stab, though, gaze for gaze!
God shield them sharply from the begger-bold!
The noxious needy ones whose battle's bald
Nonetheless for being voiceless, hits one down.
               But it's all so bad! and entirely too much for
       them.

The stench; the urine, cabbage, and dead beans,
Dead porridges of assorted dusty grains,
The old smoke, *heavy* diapers, and, they're told,
Something called chitterlings. The darkness. Drawn
Darkness, or dirty light. The soil that stirs.
The soil that looks the soil of centuries.
And for that matter the general oldness. Old
Wood. Old marble. Old tile. Old old old.
Not homekind Oldness! Not Lake Forest, Glencoe.
Nothing is sturdy, nothing is majestic,
There is no quiet drama, no rubbed glaze, no
Unkillable infirmity of such
A tasteful turn as lately they have left,
Glencoe, Lake Forest, and to which their cares
Must presently restore them. When they're done
With dullards and distortions of this fistic
Patience of the poor and put-upon.
                    They've never seen such a make-do-ness as
Newspaper rugs before! In this, this "flat,"
Their hostess is gathering up the oozed, the rich
Rugs of the morning (tattered! the bespattered. . . .)
Readies to spread clean rugs for afternoon.
Here is a scene for you. The Ladies look,
In horror, behind a substantial citizeness
Whose trains clank out across her swollen heart.
Who, arms akimbo, almost fills a door.
All tumbling children, quilts dragged to the floor
And tortured thereover, potato peelings, soft-
Eyed kitten, hunched-up, haggard, to-be-hurt.
                    Their League is allotting largesse to the Lost.
But to put their clean, their pretty money, to put
Their money collected from delicate rose-fingers
Tipped with their hundred flawless rose-nails seems. . .
                    They own Spode, Lowestoft, candelabra,
Mantels, and hostess gowns, and sunburst clocks,
Turtle soup, Chippendale, red satin"hangings,"
Aubussons and Hattie Carnegie. They Winter
In Palm Beach; cross the Water in June; attend,
When suitable, the nice Art Institute;

Buy the right books in the best bindings; saunter
On Michigan, Easter mornings, in sun or wind.
Oh Squalor! This sick four-story hulk, this fibre
With fissures everywhere! Why, what are bringings
Of loathe-love largesse? What shall peril hungers
So old old, what shall flatter the desolate?
Tin can, blocked fire escape and chitterling
And swaggering seeking youth and the puzzled wreckage
Of the middle passage, and urine and stale shames
And, again, the porridges of the underslung
And children children children. Heavens! That
Was a rat, surely, off there, in the shadows? Long
And long-tailed? Gray? The Ladies from the Ladies'
Betterment League agree it will be better
To achieve the outer air that rights and steadies,
To hie to a house that does not holler, to ring
Bells elsetime, better presently to cater
To no more Possibilities, to get
Away. Perhaps the money can be posted.
Perhaps they two may choose another Slum!
Some serious sooty half-unhappy home!–
Where loathe-love likelier may be invested.
                    Keeping their scented bodies in the center
Of the hall as they walk down the hysterical hall,
They allow their lovely skirts to graze no wall,
Are off at what they manage of a canter
And, resuming all the clues of what they were,
Try to avoid inhaling the laden air.

# ROBERT DUNCAN [Born 1919]

Born in Oakland, California, Robert Duncan was adopted by a family named Symmes at the age of one (indeed, his early poetry was written under that surname). From 1936 to 1938, Duncan studied at the University of California, Berkeley, and went on to edit two magazines: *The Experimental Review* (with Sanders Russell) and *Phoenix*. He served for a time in the army but in 1941 was given a psychiatric discharge. Between 1945 and 1950, Kenneth Rexroth exerted a mentor-like influence on Duncan. During this time, Duncan returned to study at Berkeley and for several years edited the *Berkeley Miscellany*. It was also during this period that he published such volumes as *Heavenly City, Earthly City* (1947), *Poems 1948-1949*, and *Medieval Scenes* (1950). Subsequently, he allied himself with the Black Mountain poets (Charles Olson, Robert Creeley, Denise Levertov) who, inspired by the work of William Carlos Williams, were pursuing an unfettered, non-formalistic poetic style they felt would allow for the truest representation of human experience. Some of Duncan's finest verse was produced in the sixties; in addition, he has published many essays and even a book for children, entitled *The Cat and the Blackbird*.

*King Haydn of Miami Beach*

1

In the rustling shelter of Japanese peach
with the blacks and the plum-colord lady apes
dances King Haydn of Miami Beach
the now, the now, of never perhaps,
bows to Death, bows to Death,
plans next week wonderfully pretend
a temporary pleasurable boat-trip & ride
round the capes, round the capes,
and back again.

2

King Haydn abandons the dance of his do.
With joy he resumes
the half-waltz and rumba of never
come true. But
Mr Responsible Person
booms in the head of Mr Do Why.
Love-waltz and rumba come
stop.
King Haydn abandons
the never come true.
Hops.
To the tune of Mr Do Why
vacations and oceans grow tired and die.

Fixt with a joyless partner motion
King Haydn and Mr
Dandruff Why
do the why do do why do.

### 3. Paradise Club

This is the Heaven-House Everyday Do
that Mr Responsible Person God
built in a day.

This is Mr Responsible Who
looks out for the welfare of me and you,
of Eve, of you, of Adam, of me.
This is the Absolute Person we fear.
This is His hot round biggish sun.
This is the middle of next year.
This is the bird on its wounded wing
that fell out of Heaven and started to sing,
that fell into soul, into single
extraordinary badly and poor.

This is the Other Place, the Miami Beach lure,
beyond the Absolute Door of Why
where each fallen birdie is six feet high.

This is the eye of Mr Responsible,
the Comprehensible,
sees each birdling that falles from grace
lose wits, lose form, lose time and face.
This is Mr Responsible Person.
This is His ordinary only Heaven.
King Haydn in the Other Place
dances away his chance for grace.

### 4. Psychoanalysis

Death is a sin, Death is a sin,
leaves a taste after of oil and tin.
In the fiery hell of Miami beach
the sun can glare like a red hot peach
but the night comes in
and the life goes out.
The boys and the girls play Turn About.
King Haydn and Mr Why begin

## Roots and Branches

Sail, Monarchs, rising and falling
orange merchants in spring's flowery markets!
messengers of March in warm currents of news floating,
    flitting into areas of aroma,
tracing out of air unseen roots and branches of sense
    I share in thought,
filaments woven and broken where the world might light
    casual certainties of me. There are

    echoes of what I am in what you perform
this morning. How you perfect my spirit!
    almost restore
an imaginary tree of the living in all its doctrines
    by fluttering about,
intent and easy as you are, the profusion of you!
awakening transports of an inner view of things.

## What Do I Know of the Old Lore?

A young editor wants me to write on Kabbalah for his magazine.

What do I know of the left and the right, of the Shekinah, of the
    Metatron?
It is an old book lying on the velvet cloth, the color of olive
    under-leaf and plumstain in the velvet;
it is a romance of pain and relief from pain, a tale told of the
    Lord of the Hour of Midnight,
the changing over that is a going down into Day from the Mountain.

Ah! the seed that lies in the sweetness of the Kabbalah
is the thought of those rabbis rejoicing in their common devotions,
of the thousand threads of their threnodies, praises, wisdoms,
    shared loves and curses interwoven.

There are terrible things in the design they weave, fair and unfair
    establisht in one.
How all righteousness is founded upon Jacob's cheat upon cheat,

and
    the devout
pray continually for the humiliation and defeat of Esau,
for everlasting terror and pain to eat at the nephilim.

The waves of the old jews talking
persist at the shores.

O, I know nothing of the left and the right.

The moon that moves the waters
comes clear from the earth's shadow.

All the old fears have been drawn up into the mountain that comes
    of knowing.

It is an old book of stories, the Bible is an old book of stories
–a mirror made by goblins for that Ice Queen, the Shekinah–
a likelihood of our hearts withheld from healing.

A young editor wants me to write on Kabbalah for his magazine.

Yes, for I too loved the scene of dark magic, the sorcerer's
    sending up clouds of empire and martyrdom,
the Gem made by goblins yielding its secret gold to the knowing,
enchantresses coming in to the lodestone, the star
that Adam dreams, angels
in their goblin splendors of eyes and fires
left and right ascending the ladders of letters,

El Eljon walking in the cool of His garden
–that must be all stones and gold, radioactive flowings,
molten glasses of the old volcano;

for the Kabbalah does not praise artichokes,
nor the emerald of lettuce that has a light.

What do I know of the left and the right,
who have a left hand and a right hand?

Do I put my left foot forward?

The Rabbis stop under the lemon tree
rejoicing in the cool of its leaves
which they say is the cool of the leaves of that Tree of Trees.

Look, Rabbi Eleazer says,
the Glory of the Shekinah shines from lettuces
in the Name of that Garden!


*Doves*


On June 8, 1961, news came that H.D. had had a stroke. In July Norman
Pearson wrote: "The part of the brain which controls speech has been
injured, so that she cannot recall appropriate words at will. Yet she does
have fiercely the desire to communicate, and strikes her breast in pas-
sionate frustration when there is no word at her tongue's tip. Sometimes
whole sentences will come; sometimes, everything but the key word. So
it is 'I want . . .' but one can never tell what it is she wants."

1

Mother of mouthings,
the grey doves in your many branches
code and decode what warnings
we call recall of love's watery tones?

    hurrrrrr
    harrrrrr
    hurrr

She raises the bedroom window
to let in the air and pearl-grey
    light of morning
where the first world stript of its names extends,
where initial things go,
beckoning dove-sounds recur
    taking what we know of them

from the soul leaps to the tongue's tip
     as if to tell
               what secret
in the word for it.


2


The birds claws scraping the ledges.
I hear the rustling of wings. Is it evening?
The woodwinds chortling or piping,
sounds settling down in the dark pit where the orchestra lights
glow
as the curtain rises, and in the living room,
at another stage,
lamps are lit.


3


The lady in the shade of the boughs
held a dove in her two hands,
let it fly up from the bowl she made
as if a word had left her lips.

Now that the song has flown
the tree shakes, rustling in the wind,
with no stars of its own,
for all the nets of words are gone.

The lady holds nothing in her two hands
cupt. The catches of the years are torn.
And the wood-light floods and overflows
the bowl she holds like a question.

Voices of children from playgrounds come
sounding on the wind without names.

We cannot tell who they are there
we once were too under what star?

Before words, after words . hands
lifted as a bowl for water, alms or prayer.
For what we heard was no more than a dove's

    hurrrrrr
    hurrrrrr
    hurrr

       where the Day slept
after noon, in the light's blur and shade
the Queen of the Tree's Talking
hears only the leaf sound,
whirrr of wings in the boughs,

the voices in the wind verging into leaf sound.

4

I wanted to say something,
that my heart had such a burden,
or needed a burden in order to say something.

Take what mask to find words
and as an old man come forward
into a speech he had long waited for,

had on the tip of his tongue,
from which now . O fateful thread!
Sentence that thru my song most moved!

Now from your courses the flame has fled
making but words of what I loved.

## *Bending the Bow*

We've our business to attend Day's duties,
bend back the bow in dreams as we may
til the end rimes in the taut string
with the sending. Reveries are rivers and flow
where the cold light gleams reflecting the window upon the
    surface of the table,
the presst-glass creamer, the pewter sugar bowl, the litter
    of coffee cups and saucers,
        carnations painted growing upon whose surfaces. The whole
    composition of surfaces leads into the other
            current disturbing
what I would take hold of. I'd been

in the course of a letter–I am still
in the course of a letter–to a friend,
who comes close in to my thought so that
the day is hers. My hand writing here
there shakes in the currents of . . . of air?
of an inner anticipation of . . . ? reaching to touch
ghostly exhilarations in the thought of her.
          At the extremity of this
             design
"there is a connexion working in both directions, as in
          the bow and the lyre"–
only in that swift fulfillment of the wish
          that sleep
        can illustrate my hand
          sweeps the string.

You stand behind the where-I-am.
The deep tones and shadows I will call a woman.
The quick high notes . . . You are a girl there too,
    having something of sister and of wife,
          inconsolate,
and I would play Orpheus for you again,

recall the arrow or song
to the trembling daylight
from which it sprang.


*Shadows*

Passages 11

The grail broken,
the light gone from the glass,

we would make it

anew.

From the thought of the smasht gold or silver cup

once raised to lips,

we would raise *shadows* to hold the blood the drinkers

desire so    •    that now

my fellow poets    Blaser, Spicer, Turnbull    tell

the beads of that story again,

raise hallows    as if there were a land . . .

There was a land and a time in which we were.

Where the poem would kneel    an ake    rose in my knees,

and the poem knelt in the rosy light of the ake

so that where the cup was raised up

as if the air had lips,

in the shade of my words raised,

in the flame of my words raised,

my mind worried about the sullen ake,

the hot sun

raising a fever where I lay sweating in the room.

Was it forewarning of some disease? a

painful core of the body's aging?   The ear

catches rime like pangs of disease from the air.   Was it

sign of a venereal infection raging in the blood?   For poetry

is a contagion   •   And Lust a lord

who'll find the way to make words ake and take on

heat and glow.


There is a land and a time–Morgan le Fay's–

marsh and river country,   her smoky strand

in whose lewd files I too have passt   •   to

tell the beads of that story again.


There appeard to him such a one as he hunted for,

a beast of golden hue and antlerd crown,

led on, as it were bound by a false word, to search

the maiden carrying the bleeding head

commands.    Lady whose bright laughter

rings avid,    and my heart dismays   •   For I

*dread me sore to pass this forest.*


The feverish youth    challenges the red man

who throws him down,    where he is,

(he takes his head off)

He turns aside,    face into the heat,    groaning

The while   •    They brought forth

certain wonders he did not remember what

and among those shadows

the shadowy cup passt.

## RICHARD WILBUR   [Born 1921]

Richard Wilbur was born in New York City, to a family that included editors, publishers, and artists; he grew up in rural New Jersey. While attending Amherst College he edited the school newspaper. During the Second World War, he served for two years in the 36th Infantry Division in Italy and France. Returning to the United States, he continued his education at Harvard University, where he received an M.A. Subsequently, he taught at Harvard, Wellesley, Wesleyan, and Smith. Wilbur is most comfortable writing in traditional forms and meters; his early volumes of verse include *The Beautiful Changes* (1947) and *Ceremony* (1950). In 1957, his *Things of This World* was awarded the Pulitzer Prize for poetry. In addition to his verse, Wilbur has produced several works of criticism, and his translations of the satirical comedies of Molière have received much acclaim and are often performed. Wilbur also was one of the collaborating lyricists for the Hellman-Bernstein musical version of Voltaire's *Candide*. Throughout his career he has given many readings of his works and participated energetically in the contemporary literary scene.

## Water Walker

There was an infidel who
Walked past all churches crying,
Yet wouldn't have changed his tears,
Not for the smoothest-worn pew;
You've seen
Caddis flies walking on spring-surface, water walkers who breathe
Air and know water, with weakly wings
Drying to pelt and sheen;

There is something they mean

By breaking from water and flying
Lightly some hours in air,
Then to the water-top dropping,
Floating their heirs and dying:
It's like
Paulsaul the Jew born in Tarshish, who when at bay on the steps
With Hebrew intrigued those Jewsotted Jews
Crowding to stone and strike;

Always alike and unlike,

Walking the point where air
Mists into water, and knowing
Both, with his breath, to be real,
Roman he went everywhere:
I've been
Down in Virginia at night, I remember an evening door
A table lamp lit; light stretched on the lawn,
Seeming to ask me in;

I thought if I should begin

To enter entirely that door,
Saying, "I am a son of this house,
My birth and my love are here,"
I might never come forth any more:

Air mists
Into water, past odors of halls and the fade of familial voices,
Stair creaks, piano tones falling on rugs,
Wallpaper palimpsests:

Armored the larva rests

Dreaming the streambottom tides,
Writhing at times to respire, and
Sealing to him flat stones,
He closely abides, abides:
One night
I sat till dawn on a porch, rocked in a cane-bottom chair,
In Geneseo, in Illinois,
Rocking from light to light;

Silent and out of sight

I saw the houses sleep,
And the autos beside them sleeping,
The neat plots, the like trustful houses,
Minute, armoreal, deep;
Wind went
Tamely and samely as puppies, tousling the Japanese maples,
Lawnsprays and tricycles waited for sun,
Shyly things said what they meant:

An old man stitching a tent

Could have been Saul in Tharsos,
Loved and revered; instead
He carried Jew visions to Greeks
For adoration or curses;
For he
Troubled them; whether they called him "babbler" or hailed him
                                                    "Mercurios"

(Scarcely restrained from killing him oxen),
His wasn't light company:

Still pearled with water, to be

Ravished by air makes him grow
Stranger to both, and discover
Heaven and hell in the poise
Betwixt "inhabit" and "know";
I hold
Here in my head Maine's bit speech, lithe laughter of Mobile blacks,
Opinions of salesmen, ripe tones of priests,
Plaints of the bought and sold:

Can I rest and observe unfold

The imminent singletax state,
The Negro rebellion, the rise
Of the nudist cult, the return
Of the Habsburgs, watch and wait
And praise
The spirit and not the cause, and neatly precipitate
What is not doctrine, what is not bound
To enclosured ground; what stays?

Lives that the caddis fly lays

Twixt air and water, must lie
Long under water–how Saul
Cursed once the market babblers,
Righteous could watch them die!
Who learns
How hid the trick is of justice, cannot go home, nor can leave,
But the dilemma, cherished, tyrannical,
While he despairs and burns

Da capo da capo returns.

## On the Eyes of an SS Officer

I think of Amundsen, enormously bit
By arch-dark flurries on the ice plateaus,
An amorist of violent virgin snows
At the cold end of the world's spit.

Or a Bombay saint asquat in the market place,
Eyes gone from staring the sun over the sky,
Who still dead-reckons that acetylene eye,
An eclipsed mind in a blind face.

But this one's iced or ashen eyes devise,
Foul purities, in flesh their wilderness,
Their fire; I ask my makeshift God of this
My opulent bric-a-brac earth to damn his eyes.

## The Peace of Cities

Terrible streets, the manichee hell of twilight
Glides like a giant bass between your windows,

Dark deploying in minnows into your alleys
Stirs and hushes the reefs of scudding trash.

Withinwalls voices, past the ports and locks,
Murmur below the shifting of crockery

I know not what; the barriered day expires
In scattered sounds of dread inconsequence.

Ah, this is no andante, there will come
No primavera, there was a louder and deeper

Peace in those other cities, when silver fear
Drove the people to fields, and there they heard

The Luftwaffe waft what let the sunshine in
And blew the bolt from everybody's door.

## In A Bird Sanctuary

Because they could not give it too much ground
they closely planted it with fir and shrub.
A plan of pathways, voted by the Club,
contrived to lead the respiter around
a mildly wandring wood, still at no cost
to get him lost.

Now over dear Miss Drury's favored trees
they flutter (birds) and either stop or not,
as if they were unconscious that the spot
is planned for them, and meant to buy release
for one restrained department of the soul,
to "make men whole."

It's hard to tell the purpose of a bird;
for relevance it does not seem to try.
No line can trace no flute exemplify
its traveling; it darts without the word.
Who wills devoutly to absorb, contain,
birds give him pain.

Commissioners of Public Parks have won
a partial wisdom, know that birds exist.
And seeing people equally insist
on birds and statues, they go hire a man
to swab sans rancor dung from granite stare
and marble hair.

BIRDS HAVE BEEN SEEN IN TOWERS AND ON ISLES;
ALSO ON PRIVY TOPS, IN FANEUIL HALL;
BIRDS HAVE SOME OF THEM NOT BEEN SEEN AT ALL;
BIRDS, IF THEY CARE TO, WALK ALONG IN FILE.
BIRDS DO NOT FEEL ESPECIALLY GOOD IN FLIGHT:
LET'S TREAT THEM RIGHT!

The liberty of any things becomes
the liberty of all. It also brings

their abolition into anythings.
In order's name let's not turn down our thumbs
on routine visions; we must figure out
what all's about.


### A Dutch Courtyard

What wholly blameless fun
To stand and look at pictures. Ah, they are
Immune to us. This courtyard may appear
To be consumed with sun,

Most mortally to burn,
Yet it is quite beyond the reach of eyes
Or thoughts, this place and moment oxidize;
This girl will never turn,

Cry what you dare, but smiles
Tirelessly toward the seated cavalier,
Who will not proffer you his pot of beer;
And your most lavish wiles

Can never turn this chair
To proper uses, nor your guile evict
These tenants. What surprising strict
Propriety! In despair,

Consumed with greedy ire,
Old Andrew Mellon glowered at this Dutch
Courtyard, until it bothered him so much
He bought the thing entire.


### My Father Paints the Summer

A smoky rain riddles the ocean plains,
Rings on the beaches' stones, stomps in the swales,
Batters the panes

Of the shore hotel, and the hoped-for summer chills and fails.
The summer people sigh,
"Is this July?"

They talk by the lobby fire but no one hears
For the thrum of the rain. In the dim and sounding halls,
Din at the ears,
Dark at the eyes well in the head, and the ping-pong balls
Scatter their hollow knocks
Like crazy clocks.

But up in his room by artificial light
My father paints the summer, and his brush
Tricks into sight
The prosperous sleep, the girdling stir and clear steep hush
Of a summer never seen,
A granted green.

Summer, luxuriant Sahara, the orchard spray
Gales in the Eden trees, the knight again
Can cast away
His burning mail, Rome is at Anzio: but the rain
For the ping-pong's optative bop
Will never stop.

Caught Summer is always an imagined time.
Time gave it, yes, but time out of any mind.
There must be prime
In the heart to beget that season, to reach past rain and find
Riding the palest days
Its perfect blaze.

### Sunlight Is Imagination

Each shift you make in the sunlight somewhere
Cleaves you away into dark. Now
You are clarion hair, bright brow,
Lightcaped shoulder and armside here, and there

Gone into meadow shadow. Where
Are my eyes to run?
Shall I say you are fair
In the sun,
Or mermaid you in the grass waving away?

Shall I say
    The whole green day builds hither to lift
    This flare of your hair?, I wielding such sight
    As did Juan Ponce, climbing to light
    On a morning of the Feast of the Resurrection. Aloft
    On the ocean shelf he saw the soft
    Signals of trees
    And gulls, and the sift
    Of the sea's
    Long landward airs offering trails to him.

And dim
    Each flower of Florida, but all
    Was shining; parrots prophesied;
    Vines ciphered; to each waterside
    Paths pitched in hopes to the fair and noble well
    Of sweetest savor and reflaire
    Whose ghostly taste
    And cleanse repair
    All waste,
    And where was ageless power from the first.

Yet thirst
    Makes deserts, barrens to a sign
    Deckled and delicate arbors, bleeds
    The rose, parches the prodigal seeds
    That spring toward time in air, and breaks the spine
    Of the rock. No; I shall resign
    That power, and crave
    Kindly to pine
    And to save
    The sprout and the ponderation of the land.

My hand
    Can touch but mysteries, and each
    Of a special shadow. I shall spare
    The larch its shattering ghost, the pear
    Its dark awaiter too, for shades beseech
    Originals: they running reach
    On windy days
    To touch, to teach
    What stays
    Is changed, and shadows die into dying things.

Now swings
    The sky to noon, and mysteries run
    To cover; let our love not blight
    The various world, but trust the flight
    Of love that falls again where it begun.
    All creatures are, and are undone.
    Then lose them, lose
    With love each one,
    And choose
    To welcome love in the lively wasting sun.

&

A slopeshouldered shape from scurrying burdens
Backward and forth, or perhaps a lyre
Or a clef wrung wry in tuning untunable tones,
Or a knot for tugging an out-of-hand

Vine to the trellis in clerical gardens:
Sweetness & light, ice & fire,
Nature & art have dissocketed all your bones,
Porter, poor pander ampersand.


*The Beautiful Changes*

One wading a Fall meadow finds on all sides
The Queen Anne's Lace lying like lilies

On water; it glides
So from the walker, it turns
Dry grass to a lake, as the slightest shade of you
Valleys my mind in fabulous blue Lucernes.

The beautiful changes as a forest is changed
By a chameleon's tuning his skin to it;
As a mantis, arranged
On a green leaf, grows
Into it, makes the leaf leafier, and proves
Any greenness is deeper than anyone knows.

Your hands hold roses always in a way that says
They are not only yours; the beautiful changes
In such kind ways,
Wishing ever to sunder
Things and thing's selves for a second finding, to lose
For a moment all that it touches back to wonder.

### Five Women Bathing in Moonlight

When night believes itself alone
It is most natural, conceals
No artifice. The open moon
With webs in sky and water wields

The slightest wave. This vision yields
To a cool accord of semblance, land
Leasing each wave the palest peals
Of bright apparent notes of sand.

The bathers whitely come and stand.
Water diffuses them, their hair
Like seaweed slurs the shoulders, and
Their voices in the moonstrung air

Go plucked of words. Now wading where
The moon's misprision salves them in-

To silver, they are unaware
How lost they are when they begin

To mix with water, making then
Gestures of blithe obedience,
As five Danilovas within
The soft compulsions of their dance.

## Beowulf

The land was overmuch like scenery,
The flowers attentive, the grass too garrulous green;
In the lake a dropped kerchief could be seen
The lark's reflection after the lark was gone;
The Roman road lay paved too shiningly
For a road so many men had traveled on.

Also the people were strange, were strangely warm.
The king recalled the father of his guest,
The queen brought mead in a studded cup, the rest
Were kind, but in all was a vagueness and a strain,
Because they lived in a land of daily harm.
And they said the same things again and again.

It was a childish country; and a child,
Grown monstrous, so beseiged them in the night
That all their daytimes were a dream of fright
That it would come and own them to the bone.
The hero, to his battle reconciled,
Promised to meet that monster all alone.

So then the people wandered to their sleep
And left him standing in the echoed hall.
They heard the rafters rattle fit to fall,
The child departing with a broken groan,
And found their champion in a rest so deep
His head lay harder sealed than any stone.

The land was overmuch like scenery,
The lake gave up the lark, but now its song
Fell to no ear, the flowers too were wrong,
The day was fresh and pale and swiftly old,
The night put out no smiles upon the sea;
And the people were strange, the people strangely cold.

They gave him horse and harness, helmet and mail,
A jeweled shield, an ancient battle-sword,
Such gifts as are the hero's hard reward
And bid him do again what he has done.
These things he stowed beneath his parting sail,
And wept that he could share them with no son.

He died in his own country a kinless king,
A name heavy with deeds, and mourned as one
Will mourn for the frozen year when it is done.
They buried him next the sea on a thrust of land:
Twelve men rode round his barrow all in a ring,
Singing of him what they could understand.


### Still, Citizen Sparrow

Still, citizen sparrow, this vulture which you call
Unnatural, let him but lumber again to air
Over the rotten office, let him bear
The carrion ballast up, and at the tall

Tip of the sky lie cruising. Then you'll see
That no more beautiful bird is in heaven's height,
No wider more placid wings, no watchfuller flight;
He shoulders nature there, the frightfully free,

The naked-headed one. Pardon him, you
Who dart in the orchard aisles, for it is he
Devours death, mocks mutability,
Has heart to make an end, keeps nature new.

Thinking of Noah, childheart, try to forget
How for so many bedlam hours his saw
Soured the song of birds with its wheezy gnaw,
And the slam of his hammer all the day beset

The people's ears. Forget that he could bear
To see the towns like coral under the keel,
And the fields so dismal deep. Try rather to feel
How high and weary it was, on the waters where

He rocked his only world, and everyone's.
Forgive the hero, you who would have died
Gladly with all you knew; he rode that tide
To Ararat; all men are Noah's sons.

## The Pardon

My dog lay dead five days without a grave
In the thick of summer, hid in a clump of pine
And a jungle of grass and honeysuckle-vine.
I who had loved him while he kept alive

Went only close enough to where he was
To sniff the heavy honeysuckle-smell
Twined with another odor heavier still
And hear the flies' intolerable buzz.

Well, I was ten and very much afraid.
In my kind world the dead were out of range
And I could not forgive the sad or strange
In beast or man. My father took the spade

And buried him. Last night I saw the grass
Slowly divide (it was the same scene
But now it glowed a fierce and mortal green)
And saw the dog emerging. I confess

I felt afraid again, but still he came
In the carnal sun, clothed in a hymn of flies,
And death was breeding in his lively eyes.
I started in to cry and call his name,

Asking forgiveness of his tongueless head.
. . . I dreamt the past was never past redeeming:
But whether this was false or honest dreaming
I beg death's pardon now. And mourn the dead.


### Ceremony

A striped blouse in a clearing by Bazille
Is, you may say, a patroness of boughs
Too queenly kind toward nature to be kin.
But ceremony never did conceal,
Save to the silly eye, which all allows,
How much we are the woods we wander in.

Let her be some Sabrina fresh from stream,
Lucent as shallows slowed by wading sun,
Bedded on fern, the flowers' cynosure:
Then nymph and wood must nod and strive to dream
That she is airy earth, the trees, undone,
Must ape her languor natural and pure.

Ho-hum. I am for wit and wakefulness,
And love this feigning lady by Bazille.
What's lightly hid is deepest understood,
And when with social smile and formal dress
She teaches leaves to curtsey and quadrille,
I think there are most tigers in the wood.

*Pangloss's Song*

I

Dear boy, you will not hear me speak
    With sorrow or with rancor
Of what has paled my rosy cheek
    And blasted it with canker;
'Twas Love, great Love, that did the deed
    Through Nature's gentle laws,
And how should ill effects proceed
    From so divine a cause?

Sweet honey comes from bees that sting,
    As you are well aware;
To one adept in reasoning,
Whatever pains disease may bring
Are but the tangy seasoning
    To Love's delicious fare.

II

Columbus and his men, they say,
    Conveyed the virus hither
Whereby my features rot away
    And vital powers wither;
Yet had they not traversed the seas
    And come infected back,
Why, think of all the luxuries
    That modern life would lack!

All bitter things conduce to sweet,
    As this example shows;
Without the little spirochete
We'd have no chocolate to eat,
Nor would tobacco's fragrance greet
    The European nose.

### III

Each nation guards its native land
   With cannon and with sentry,
Inspectors look for contraband
   At every port of entry,
Yet nothing can prevent the spread
   Of Love's divine disease:
It rounds the world from bed to bed
   As pretty as you please.

Men worship Venus everywhere,
   As plainly may be seen;
The decorations which I bear
Are nobler than the Croix de Guerre,
And gained in service of our fair
   And universal Queen.

# INDEX

Poet names are in bold face; poem titles are in italics; and poem first lines are enclosed in quotation marks.

# ACKNOWLEDGEMENTS

Permission to reprint copyrighted poems is gratefully acknowledged to the following:

OWEN DODSON, for "Six O'Clock" and "Mary Passed This Morning". Copyright © by Owen Dodson.

DOUBLEDAY & COMPANY, INC., for "The Coming of the Cold"; "The Auction" from *The Collected Poems of Theodore Roethke* by Theodore Roethke. Copyright © 1941 by Theodore Roethke. "Lull"; "Highway: Michigan" from *The Collected Works of Theodore Roethke* by Theodore Roethke. Copyright © 1940 by Theodore Roethke. "Orchids"; "Transplanting" from *The Collected Works of Theodore Roethke* by Theodore Roethke. Copyright © 1948 by Theodore Roethke. "Moss-Gathering" from *The Collected Works of Theodore Roethke* by Theodore Roethke. Copyright © 1946 by Editorial Publications, Inc. "Big Wind" from *The Collected Works of Theodore Roethke* by Theodore Roethke. Copyright © 1947 by the United Chapters of Phi Beta Kappa. "Frau Bauman, Frau Schmidt and Frau Schwartze" from *The Collected Works of Theodore Roethke* by Theodore Roethke. Copyright © 1952 by Theodore Roethke. "My Papa's Waltz" from *The Collected Works of Theodore Roethke* by Theodore Roethke. Copyright © 1942 by Hearst Magazine, Inc. "The Lost Son"; "The Shape of Fire" from *The Collected Works of Thoedore Roethke* by Theodore Roethke. Copyright © 1947 by Theodore Roethke. "Where Knock Is Open Wide" from *The Collected Works of Theodore Roethke* by Theodore Roethke. Copyright © 1950 by Theodore Roethke. "A Walk in Late Summer" from *The Collected Works of Theodore Roethke* by Theodore Roethke. Copyright © 1957 by Theodore Roethke. "The Far Field" from *The Collected Works of Theodore Roethke* by Theodore Roethke. Copyright © 1962 by Beatrice Roethke as Administratrix of the Estate of Theodore Roethke.

ROBERT DUNCAN, for "King Hadyn of Miami Beach". Copyright © by Robert Duncan.

FARRAR, STRAUS & GIROUX, INC., for "The Map"; "The Imaginary Iceberg"; "The Man-Moth"; "The Monument"; "Florida"; "The Fish"; "A Cold Spring" and "Questions of Travel" from *The Complete Poems Of Elizabeth Bishop*. Copyright © 1933, 1935, 1936, 1937, 1938, 1939, 1940, 1941, 1944, 1945, 1946, 1947, 1948, 1949, 1951, 1952, 1955, 1956, 1957, 1958, 1959, 1960, 1961, 1962, 1963, 1964, 1965, 1966, 1967, 1968, 1969, 1971, 1972, 1973, 1974, 1975, 1976 by Elizabeth Bishop. Renewal copyright © 1967, 1968, 1971, 1973, 1974, 1975, 1976, 1979 by Elizabeth Bishop. Renewal copyright © 1980 by Alice Helen Methfessel. Copyright © 1983 by Alice Helen Methfessel. Dream Songs # 1, 5, 14, 15, 18, 22, 75, 76, 121, 149, 162 from *The Dream Songs* by John Berryman. Copyright © 1959, 1962, 1963, 1964, 1965, 1966, 1967, 1968, 1969 by John Berryman. 17–39 Excerpt from *Homage To Mistress Bradstreet* by John Berryman. Copyright © 1956 by John Berryman. Copyright renewed © 1984 by Mrs. Kate Berryman. "The Quaker Graveyard in Nantucket"; "The Drunken Fisher Man"; "At the Indian Killer's Grave"; "After the Surprising Conversations"; "Where the Rainbow Ends"; "To Delmore Schwartz"; "My Last Afternoon with Uncle Devereux Winslow" and "Father's Bedroom" by Robert Lowell. Copyright © 1944, 1946, 1947, 1950, 1951, 1956, 1960, 1961, 1962, 1963, 1964, 1965, 1966, 1967, 1968, 1969, 1970, 1973, 1976 by Robert Lowell. "Sorrow Is the Only Faithful One" and "I Break the Sky" from *Powerful Long Ladder* by Owen Dodson. Copyright 1946, copyright renewed © 1974 by Owen Dodson. "The Knight, Death, and the Devil"; "The Venetian Blind"; "In the Ward: the Sacred Wood"; "The Death of the Ball Turret Gunner"; "Losses"; "Transient Barracks"; "Siegfried"; "Pilots, Man Your Planes"; "Burning Letters" from *The Complete Poems* by Randall Jarrell. Copyright 1944, 1945, 1949, 1957, copyright renewed © 1972, 1973, 1976 by Mrs. Randall Jarrell.

GWENDOLYN BROOKS, for "Negro Hero"; "The Lovers of the Poor" and selections from *A Street in Bronzeville*: "kichenette building"; "the mother"; "southeast corner"; "hunchback girl: she thinks of heaven"; "a song in the front yard"; "the ballad of chocolate Mabbie"; "the preacher: ruminates behind the sermon"; "Sadie and Maud"; "the independent man" and "the vacant lot" from *Selected Poems* by Gwendolyn Brooks. Copyright © 1944, 1945, 1949, 1959, 1960, 1963 by Gwendolyn Brooks.

HARCOURT BRACE JOVANOVICH, INC., for "Water Walker"; "On the Eyes of an SS Officer"; "The Peace of Cities"; "In a Bird Sanctuary"; "A Dutch Courtyard"; "My Father Paints the Summer" and "The Beautiful Changes" from *The Beautiful Changes and Other Poems* by Richard Wilbur. Copyright 1947, 1975 by Richard Wilbur. "Five Women Bathing in Moonlight"; "Beowulf"; "Still, Citizen Sparrow"; "The Pardon" and "Ceremony" from *Ceremony and Other Poems* by Richard Wilbur. Copyright 1950, 1978 by Richard Wilbur. "Pangloss's Song" from his volume *Advice To a Prophet and Other Poems* by Richard Wilbur. Copyright © 1957, 1984 by Richard Wilbur.
INDIANA UNIVERSITY PRESS, for "Headless" and "Ten Dreamers in a Motel" from *Poems 1930–1960* by Josephine Miles. Copyright © 1960 by Indiana University Press.
INTERNATIONAL CREATIVE MANAGEMENT, for "Poem Out of Childhood"; "Effort at Speech Between Two People" and "Theory of Flight" from *Theory of Flight* by Muriel Rukeyser. Copyright © 1935 and 1963 by Muriel Rukeyser. "The Speaking Tree" from *Waterlily Fire, Poems 1935–1962* by Muriel Rukeyser. Copyright © 1962 by Muriel Rukeyser.
LIVERIGHT PUBLISHING CORPORATION for "Electrical Storm"; "Full Moon"; "Belsen, Day of Liberation"; "The Ballad of Sue Ellen Westerfield"; "Night, Death, Mississippi"; "Day of the Dead"; "Market" and "Summertime and the Living . . ." from *Angle of Ascent, New and Selected Poems* by Robert Hayden. Copyright © 1975, 1972, 1970, 1966 by Robert Hayden.
MACMILLAN PUBLISHING COMPANY, for "From Venice That Afternoon" and "Forest" from *New and Selected Poems* by Jean Garrigue. Copyright 1944 by Jean Garrigue. "Primer of Plato" and "False Country of the Zoo" from *New and Selected Poems* by Jean Garrigue. Copyright 1947 by Jean Garrigue, renewed 1975 by Aileen Ward. "Gravepiece"; "The Maimed Grasshopper Speaks Up"; "Lightly Like Music Running" and "This Day Is Not Like That Day" from *New and Selected Poems* by Jean Garrigue. Copyright 1953 by Jean Garrigue, renewed 1981 by Aileen Ward. "The Hook" and Cataract" from *The World Before Us* by Theodore Weiss. Copyright 1951 by Theodore Weiss. "Preface" from *The World Before Us* by Theodore Weiss. Copyright 1952 by Theodore Weiss. "A Certain Village" from *The World Before Us* by Theodore Weiss. Copyright © 1970 by Theodore Weiss.
NEW DIRECTIONS for "Night Has Been as Beautiful as Virginia"; "A Letter on the Use of Machine Guns at Weddings"; "Under the Green Ledge"; "An Examination into Life and Death"; "Saturday Night in the Parthenon" from *The Collected Poems of Kenneth Patchen*, by Kenneth Patchen. Copyright 1936 by Kenneth Patchen, 1942 by New Directions Publishing Corporation. "Orion"; "The Illusion"; "The Impossible Choices"; "The Presence"; "The Residual Years"; "Eastward the Armies"; "Under a Keeping Spring"; "End of Summer"; "In the Dream's Recess" from *The Residual Years* by William Everson. Copyright 1948 by New Directions Publishing Corporation. "In the Naked Bed Plato's Cave"; "Father and Son"; "The Sin of Hamlet"; "Prothalamion"; "Socrates' Ghost Must Haunt Me Now"; "Calmly We Walk Through This April's Day"; "Dogs Are Shakespearean, Children Are Strangers"; "I Am to My Own Heart Merely a Serf"; "The Heavy Bear That Goes with Me"; "A Dog Named Ego, the Snowflakes as Kisses"; "During December's Death"; "Once and for All"; "Parlez-vous Francais?" from *Selected Poems: Summer Knowledge* by Delmore Schwartz. Copyright © 1954, 1955, 1958, 1959 by Delmore Schwartz. "Two British Airmen"; "The Strife Between the Poet and Ambition"; Tower of Babel"; "Lent in a Year of War"; "Aubade: Lake Erie"; "A Psalm"; "St. Malachy"; "There Has To Be a Jail for Ladies" from *The Collected Poems of Thomas Merton.* Copyright 1944, 1949 by Our Lady of Gethsemani Monastery, © 1962 by the Abbey of Gethsemani, Inc. © 1977 by the Trustees of the Merton Legacy Trust. "Roots and Branches"; "What Do I Know of the Old Lore?" and "Doves" from *Roots and Branches* by Robert Duncan. Copyright © 1964 by Robert Duncan. "Bending the Bow"; "Shadows" from *Bending the Bow* by Robert Duncan. Copyright © 1966, 1968 by Robert Duncan. "Andree Rexroth"; "Climbing Milestone Mountain, August 22nd, 1937"; "Night Below Zero"; "A Sword in a Cloud of Light" from *Collected Shorter Poems* by Kenneth Rexroth. Copyright 1944 by New Directions Publishing Corporation, Copyright © 1940, 1963 by Kenneth Rexroth.
RANDOM HOUSE, INC., for "The Lordly Hudson"; "For My Birthday, 1939"; "For Sally, with a Piano"; "Reading Adonais"; "Saint Cecilia's Day, 1941" and "General Washington" from *Collected Poems* by Paul Goodman, edited by Taylor Stoehr. Copyright © 1972, 1973 by the Estate of Paul Goodman. "Auto Wreck" and "The Fly"; copyright 1942 and renewed 1970 by Karl Shapiro. "University"; copyright 1940 and renewed 1968 by Karl Shapiro. "Troop Train"; copyright 1943 and renewed 1971 by Karl Shapiro. "The Gun"; copyright 1943 by

*CommonSense*. "Lord, I Have Seen Too Much"; copyright 1944 by Karl Shapiro. "Jew"; copyright 1943 by Karl Shapiro. "The Synagogue"; copyright 1943 and renewed 1971 by Karl Shapiro. "V-Letter"; copyright 1943 by Karl Shapiro. "Elegy for a Dead Soldier"; copyright 1944 by Karl Shapiro. "The Conscientious Objector"; copyright 1947 and renewed 1975 by Karl Shapiro. "Lower the Standard"; copyright © 1964 by Karl Shapiro. "Randall Jarrell"; © copyright 1963 by Karl Shapiro. "My Father's Funeral"; copyright © 1976 by Karl Shapiro. Reprinted from *Collected Poems 1940–1978* by Karl Shapiro.

THE UNIVERSITY OF ILLINOIS PRESS, for "Herald"; "Seer"; "Personification"; "Cat"; "Appointment in Doctor's Office"; "Romantic Letters"; "Views to See Clayton From"; "Cloud"; "Gypsy"; "Tourists" and "Lucifer Alone" from *Collected Poems 1930–1983* by Josephine Miles. Copyright 1983 by Josephine Miles.

UNIVERSITY OF NEBRASKA PRESS, for "For My Daughter"; "Aspects of Robinson"; "January"; "1926" and "Robinson" from *The Collected Poems of Weldon Kees*, edited by Donald Justice. Copyright © 1975 by the University of Nebraska Press.

WESLEYAN UNIVERSITY PRESS, for "Bowery"; "The Doctor"; "Epilogue for F.D.R."; "The Ice Cream Parlor Romance"; "Interior Dialogue"; "The Outlaw"; "Marriage" and "The Poet Is a Hospital Clerk" from *Poems 1934–1969*. Copyright © 1966, 1969 by David Ignatow.